JN087389

新装版 村上春樹ハイブ・リット

村上春樹 編・訳

柴田元幸 総合監修

Tim O'Brien
Raymond Carver
Haruki Murakami

HYB-LIT

Haruki

Murakami

アルク

Haruki Murakami Hyb-Lit
村上春樹ハイブ・リット

村上春樹 編・訳

Tim O'Brien
Raymond Carver
Haruki Murakami

装幀　松田行正＋杉本聖士

Contents 目次

翻訳の神様

　僕はいちおう小説家が本業で、翻訳は副業ということになっている。実際にそのとおりで、小説を書いているときは、何よりもまず小説の仕事を優先する。毎日早朝に起きて頭がいちばんクリアな時間に集中して小説を書いてしまう。それから食事をするか、運動をするかして、「さあ、これで今日のノルマは成し遂げた。あとは好きなことをしてもいい」というところで、おもむろに翻訳にとりかかる。

　つまり翻訳という作業は僕にとっては「仕事」というよりはむしろ、hobbyに近いものなのだ。つまりもう日課としての、責務としての仕事は終わって、（たとえば）これから魚釣りに行ってもいいし、クラリネットの練習をしてもいいし、しゃくなげのスケッチをしてもいい、何をするのも自由だというところで、それらの選択肢に進むことなく、あえて机に向かって翻訳をするわけだから、つまりそれだけ純粋に翻訳が好きなのだということになるだろう。自分で言うのもなんだけど、趣味としてはなかなか悪くないと思う（クラリネットが吹けるというのも楽しそうではあるけれど）。

　これまでずっと翻訳をやってきてよかったなあと思うことは、小説家としていくつかある。まず第一に現実問題として、小説を書きたくないときには、翻訳をしていられるということがある。エッセイのネタはそのうちに切れるけれど、翻訳のネタは切れない。それから小説を書くのと翻訳をするのとでは、使用する頭の部位が違うので、交互にやっていると脳のバランスがうまくとれてくるということもある。もうひとつは、翻訳作業を通して文章について多くを学べることだ。外国語で（僕

の場合は英語で）書かれたある作品を読んで「素晴らしい」と思う。そして
てその作品を翻訳してみる。するとその文章のどこがそんなに素晴らし
かったのかという仕組みのようなものが、より明確に見えてくる。実際
に手を動かして、ひとつの言語から別の言語に移し替えていると、その
文章をただ目で読んでいる時より、見えてくるものが遥かに多くなり、
また立体的になってくる。そしてそういう作業を長年にわたって続けて
いると、「良い文章がなぜ良いのか」という原理のようなものが自然に
わかってくる。

　そんなわけで小説家の僕にとって、翻訳という作業はいつも変わらず
大事な文章の師であったし、それと同時に気の置けない文学仲間でも
あった。僕には実際には先生もいないし、文学仲間と言えるような個人
的な友だちもいない。もう三十年近くずっと一人で小説を書いてきた。
それは長く孤独な道のりだった・・・というとあまりにも月並みな表現
になるが、まあなんというか、多くの局面において実際にそのとおり
だった。もし翻訳という「趣味」がなかったら、小説家としての僕の人
生はときとして耐え難いものになっていたかもしれない。

　そしてある時点から、僕にとっての「翻訳」は両方向に向けたモーメ
ントになっていった。僕がほかの作家の作品を日本語に翻訳するだけで
はなく、僕の書いた小説が多くの言語に翻訳されるという状況が生まれ
てきたからだ。今では42の言語に翻訳され、僕の作品を外国語で読む
読者の数は驚くほど増えている。外国を旅行して書店に入り、自分の作
品が平積みにされているのを目にすることも多くなった。それは本当に

嬉しいことだ。もちろんどんな作家にとってもそれは嬉しいことであるに違いないが、とりわけ翻訳というものに深く携わってきた僕のような人間にとって、自分の本が「翻訳書」としてそこに並んでいるのを目にするのは、実に感慨深いものがある。

　いちばん最初に外国の雑誌に売れた僕の作品は（たしか）短篇小説『TVピープル』だった。1991年のことで、それは「ニューヨーカー」に掲載された。「ニューヨーカー」は僕にとっては長いあいだまさに憧れの雑誌だったし、そんな「聖域」にも近いところに自分の作品が掲載され、名前が印刷されるなんて、にわかには信じがたいことだった。おまけに原稿料までもらえるのだ。それはどんな立派な文学賞をもらうよりも、僕には嬉しいことだった。ロサンジェルス・ドジャーズのユニフォームを着て初めてマウンドに立った野茂英雄も、程度の差こそあれ、きっと同じような気持ちを味わったのではないかという気がする。

　そのときに僕がつくづく思ったのは「世の中にはきっと翻訳の神様がいるんだ」ということだった。志賀直哉に「小僧の神様」という作品があるが、それと同じような意味合いでの個人的な神様だ。僕は自分の好きな作品を選び、僕なりに心を込めて、ひとつひとつ大事に翻訳をしてきた。まだまだ不足はあるにせよ、少しずつではあるが翻訳の腕もあがっていると思う。翻訳の神様は空の上でそれをじっとご覧になっていて、「村上もなかなかよくがんばって翻訳をしておる。このへんで少し褒美をやらなくてはな」と思われたのかもしれない。

　翻訳の神様を裏切らないためにも、これからもがんばって優れた翻訳

をしなくてはなと日々自戒している。まだ先は長いし、翻訳したい作品もたくさん残っている。そしてそれは、小説家としての僕にとってもまだまだ成長する余地が残されている、ということでもあるのだ。

　ここに収められたレイ・カーヴァーやティム・オブライエンの作品からも、翻訳作業を通して、僕は大事なことを数多く学んだ。彼らから学んだもっとも大事なものは、小説を書くということに対する姿勢の良さだったと思う。そのような姿勢の良さは、必ず文章に滲み出てくるものだ。そして読者の心を本当に惹きつけるのは、文章のうまさでもなく、筋の面白さでもなく、そのようなたたずまいなのだ。僕が心がけたのは、彼らの「姿勢の良さ」を、できるだけあるがままに率直に日本語に移し替えることだった。うまくいっているといいのだけれど。

2008年7月28日
村上春樹
※旧版より再掲

英語と文学を楽しむ『村上春樹ハイブ・リット』

編集部編／柴田元幸監修

　本書『村上春樹ハイブ・リット』のタイトルにある「ハイブ・リット」とは、hybrid（混成の）とliterature（文学）の合成語です。アメリカ短篇小説という「文学」を、❶原文、❷翻訳、❸朗読、といろいろな角度から味わうことで英語が学べる本シリーズの呼称です。ここでは、「ハイブ・リット」で英語力をアップさせる方法を目的別にお教えします。

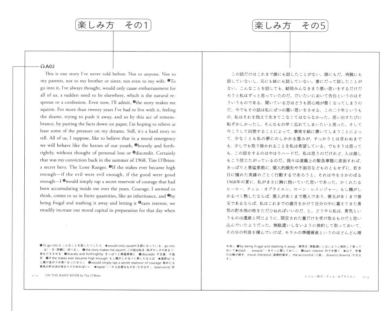

楽しみ方　その1

楽しみ方　その5

楽しみ方　その2, 3, 4

楽しみ方　その1

リーディング：物語を英語で読む

　左ページには原文の英語を掲載しています（「レーダーホーゼン」は原文が日本語のため英訳）。英語で小説を読んだことのない人も、右ページの村上春樹訳やページ下の脚注を頼りに英語のリーディングに挑戦してみましょう。本書掲載の作品は比較的平易な英語で書かれているので、読みやすく感じるはずです。自信がついたら、それぞれの短篇を収録した原書に挑戦してみては？

(楽しみ方 その2)

リスニング：物語の朗読を聞く

本書は2枚のCDに、英語の朗読を収録しています。トラック番号は収録トラック数を表わします（A01ならば、CD-Aのトラック1ということ）。「レイニー河で」は作家ティム・オブライエン自身が、そのほかの作品はアメリカ人ナレーターが朗読しています。意味の固まりを意識しながら聞くと、英語の構文の感覚を養えるでしょう。何度も繰り返し聞くことで、英語のリズムやイントネーションに慣れ、リスニング力がアップします。

(楽しみ方 その3)

リピーティング：朗読を聴いて繰り返し言ってみる

リピーティングとは1センテンスごとに音声を止め、聞こえたままにまねをして、感情を込めて英語を口に出すことです。最初から全部をリピーティングするのではなく、お気に入りのパラグラフ（段落）を選んで取り組むとよいでしょう。英語をしっかりと聞き取ることでリスニング力、そして、忠実に再生することで話し方のリズムやイントネーションを身に付けられるのでスピーキング力アップに役立ちます。

(楽しみ方 その4)

ディクテーション：朗読の英語を書き取る

朗読の音声を繰り返し聞いて、英語を書き取ります。聞いて書き取ることによって現在の英語力を認識することができます。集中して英語を聞くのでリスニング力が伸び、英語が頭に残るのでスピーキングにも活きてきます。リピーティング同様、覚えてしまいたいくらいに気に入った1パラグラフから始めるのがよいでしょう。

(楽しみ方 その5)

トランスレーション：物語を日本語に訳す

翻訳はすべて村上春樹によるものです。対訳形式なので、翻訳者がいかに英語を日本語に置き換えているかを読み比べることが可能です。物語を翻訳し、自訳と村上訳とを較べて添削することによって、より深く英語のニュアンスを理解し味わうことができます。

- 弊社制作の音声CDは、CDプレーヤーでの再生を保証する規格品です。
- パソコンでご使用になる場合、CD-ROMドライブとの相性により、ディスクを再生できない場合がございます。ご了承ください。
- パソコンでタイトル・トラック情報を表示させたい場合は、iTunesをご利用ください。iTunesでは、弊社がCDのタイトル・トラック情報を登録しているGracenote社のCDDB（データベース）からインターネットを介してトラック情報を取得することができます。
- CDとして正常に音声が再生できるディスクからパソコンやmp3プレーヤー等への取り込み時にトラブルが生じた際は、まず、そのアプリケーション（ソフト）、プレーヤーの製作元へご相談ください。

【無料】英文音声の入手・活用方法　編集部編

Story 2と3の英文音声は、以下の要領で無料でダウンロードしていただけます（Story 1は権利上配信することができません。ご了承ください）。
本サービスのご利用には、メールアドレスIDの登録／ログインが必要となります（無料）。あらかじめご了承ください。

パソコンの場合

パソコンで、音声データをダウンロードするには、以下のURLから行います。

1）アルクのダウンロードセンター
　　https://www.alc.co.jp/dl/
2）ログイン後、ダウンロードセンターで、書籍名または商品コード 7019060 でコンテンツを検索します。
3）検索後、ダウンロード用ボタンをクリックし、以下のパスワードを入力してコンテンツをダウンロードしてください。

スマートフォンの場合

スマートフォンまたはiPadに直接ダウンロードするには、無料アプリ「語学のオトモ ALCO」が必要です（ALCOインストール済みの方は3から）。iOS、Androidの両方に対応しています。再生スピードの変更や、秒数指定の巻き戻し・早送りなど、便利な機能が満載です。語学学習にぜひご活用ください。

1）ALCOのインストール
　　https://www.alc.co.jp/alco/
2）インストール後、ALCOへのログインには、メールアドレスIDの登録が必要となります（無料）。
3）ALCOにログインし、ホーム画面の下部にある「ダウンロードセンター」バーをタップします（QRコードを使えば、以下4、5の操作が不要です）。
4）ダウンロードセンターで、書籍名または商品コード 7019060 でコンテンツを検索します。
5）検索後、ダウンロード用ボタンをクリックし、以下のパスワードを入力します。個別ダウンロードページから、コンテンツをダウンロードしてください。

　　パスワード　→　haruki60

※サービスの内容は、予告なく変更する場合がございます。あらかじめご了承ください。

ON THE RAINY RIVER

by

Tim O'Brien

レイニー河で

ティム・オブライエン

　連作短篇集 *The Things They Carried*（邦題『本当の戦争の話をしよう』）のなかの一作。この作品集では、作者と同じ「ティム・オブライエン」あるいは「ティム」と名づけられた人物のベトナム戦争体験が主として語られる。が、ある短篇で語られた「事実」が別の短篇で否定されていたり、登場人物オブライエンの体験と作者オブライエン自身の体験とが微妙に食い違っていたりで、単に作者が自分の体験を素朴に綴った作品では決してない。

　とはいえ、ティム・オブライエンの文章の力強さは、語らずにはいられないことを宿命的に持ってしまった書き手が、それをどこまで生々しく伝えられるかに心を砕くことから生まれているという印象を与える。作品間で事実が食い違ったりするのも、あくまでそのための手段であるように思える。

　道義的に賛成できない戦争に徴兵された若者が、カナダに逃亡するという選択肢と、人々の後ろ指を恐れて戦争に行くという選択肢のあいだで引き裂かれるさまを、肉が転がり血が飛び散る精肉加工工場での仕事や、理解ある父親的人物とのやりとりなどを通してこの短篇は描いていく。到達点はきわめて単純だが（たとえば一番最後の二センテンスのシンプルさ）、そこに到達した時点で、「ティム・オブライエン」の体験は、彼だけが持つ独自性と、万人が共有しうる普遍性の両方を獲得している。（柴田元幸）

🎧A02

This is one story I've never told before. Not to anyone. Not to my parents, not to my brother or sister, not even to my wife. ❶To go into it, I've always thought, would only cause embarrassment for all of us, a sudden need to be elsewhere, which is the natural response to a confession. Even now, I'll admit, ❷the story makes me squirm. For more than twenty years I've had to live with it, feeling the shame, trying to push it away, and so by this act of remembrance, by putting the facts down on paper, I'm hoping to relieve at least some of the pressure on my dreams. Still, it's a hard story to tell. All of us, I suppose, like to believe that in a moral emergency we will behave like the heroes of our youth, ❸bravely and forthrightly, without thought of personal loss or ❹discredit. Certainly that was my conviction back in the summer of 1968. Tim O'Brien: a secret hero. The Lone Ranger. ❺If the stakes ever became high enough—if the evil were evil enough, if the good were good enough—I ❻would simply tap a secret reservoir of courage that had been accumulating inside me over the years. Courage, I seemed to think, comes to us in finite quantities, like an inheritance, and ❼by being frugal and stashing it away and letting it ❽earn interest, we steadily increase our moral capital in preparation for that day when

---

❶To go into it: こんなことを話したりしたら　★would only causeの主語になっている。go into ...は「〜を（詳細に）述べる」。　❷the story makes me squirm: この話は私を（恥ずかしさのあまり）身もだえさせる　❸bravely and forthrightly: きっぱりと勇猛果敢に　❹discredit: 不名誉、不面目　❺If the stakes ever became high enough: もし機がしかるべく熟したならば　★直訳は「もし賭け金が十分高くなったなら」。　❻would simply tap a secret reservoir of courage: 秘めたる勇気の貯水池の栓をただひねればいい　★tapは「（〜から必要なものを）引き出す」、reservoirは「貯

この話だけはこれまで誰にも話したことがない。誰にもだ。両親にも話していないし、兄にも妹にも話していない。妻にだって話したことがない。こんなことを話しても、結局みんなきまり悪い思いをするだけだろうと私はずっと思っていたのだ。だいたいにおいて告白というのはそういうものである。聞いている方はどうも居心地が悪くなってしまうのだ。今でもその話は私にばつの悪い思いをさせる。この二十年というもの、私はそれを抱えて生きてこなくてはならなかった。思い出すたびに恥ずかしかったし、そんなもの早く忘れてしまいたいと思った。そして今こうして回想することによって、事実を紙に書いてしまうことによって、少なくとも私の夢にのしかかる重みが、すっかりとは言わぬまでも、少しでも取り除かれることを私は希望している。でもそうは思っても、この話をするのはやはりハードだ。私は思うのだけれど、人は誰しもこう信じたがっているのだ。我々は道義上の緊急事態に直面すれば、きっぱりと勇猛果敢に、個人的損失や不面目などものともせずに、若き日に憧れた英雄のごとく行動するであろうと。それは今をさかのぼる1968年の夏に、私がまさに胸に抱いていた思いであった。かくれたるヒーロー、ティム・オブライエン。ローン・レインジャー。もし機がしかるべく熟したならば、悪人があくまで悪人であり、善玉があくまで善玉であるならば、私はこれまでの歳月をかけて自分の中に蓄えてきた勇気の貯水池の栓をただひねればいいのだ、と。どうやら私は、勇気というものは遺産と同じように、限定された量だけを受け取るものだと思い込んでいたようだった。無駄遣いしないように倹約して取っておいて、その分の利息を積んでいけば、モラルの準備資産というのはどんどん増

水池」。❼ by being frugal and stashing it away:（勇気を）無駄遣いしないように倹約して取っておいて★stash ... awayは「〜をそっと隠しておく」。❽ earn interest: 利子を稼ぐ　★以下、貯蓄の比喩が続き、moral interestは「道徳的資本」、the accountは「口座」、draw(n) downは「引き出す」。

the account must be drawn down. It was a comforting theory. **❶**It dispensed with all those bothersome little acts of daily courage; it offered hope and grace to the repetitive coward; it justified the past while amortizing the future.

🎧A03

In June of 1968, a month after graduating from Macalester College, I was drafted to fight a war I hated. I was twenty-one years old. Young, yes, and politically naive, but even so the American war in Vietnam seemed to me wrong. Certain blood was being shed for uncertain reasons. I saw no unity of purpose, no consensus on matters of philosophy or history or law. **❷**The very facts were shrouded in uncertainty: Was it a civil war? A war of national liberation or simple **❸**aggression? Who started it, and when, and why? What really happened to **❹**the USS *Maddox* on that dark night in the Gulf of Tonkin? Was Ho Chi Minh a Communist **❺**stooge, or a nationalist savior, or both, or neither? What about **❻**the Geneva Accords? What about **❼**SEATO and the Cold War? What about **❽**dominoes? America was divided on these and a thousand other issues, and the debate had spilled out across the floor of the United States Senate and into the streets, and smart men **❾**in pinstripes could not agree on even the most fundamental matters of public policy. The only certainty that summer was moral confusion. It was my view then,

---

❶It dispensed with all those bothersome little acts of daily courage: そのおかげで、勇気を必要とする煩雑でささやかな日常的行為なしで済ませることができた　**❷**The very facts were shrouded in uncertainty: 事実そのものが不確かさという衣に覆われていた　★be shrouded in . . .は「～に包まれている」。**❸**aggression: (他国への) 侵略　**❹**the USS *Maddox*: 駆逐艦マドック ス　★ヴェトナム戦争当時、1964年に米軍艦のマドックスとターナー・ジョイが、トンキン湾で北ヴェトナムから攻撃された (トンキン湾事件)。この事件を口実にして米軍の北ヴェトナムへの空海

加していくし、それをある日必要になったときにさっと引き出せばいいのだと。それはまったく虫の良い理論だった。そのおかげで私は、勇気を必要とする煩雑でささやかな日常的行為をどんどんパスすることができた。そういう常習的卑怯さに対して、その理論は希望と赦免を与えてくれた。将来に向けて積み立てているんだからということで、過去は正当化された。

　1968年の六月、マカレスター・カレッジを卒業した一カ月後に、私は徴兵された。その戦争を私は憎んでいた。私は当時二十一歳だった。そう、私は若かったし、政治的にはナイーヴであったけれど、それでも私はヴェトナムにおけるアメリカの戦争は間違ったものであるように思えた。確かならざる大義のために、確かな血が流されていた。私の目には統一された目的が見えなかったし、哲学的、歴史的、法律的な問題をとってみても、そこにコンセンサスが存在するとは思えなかった。ありのままの事実は不確かさという衣に覆われていた。それは内戦なのか、それは民族の解放戦争なのか、それともただの単純な侵略戦争なのか。誰がいつどんな理由でそれを始めたのか。闇夜のトンキン湾で、駆逐艦マドックスに実際に何が起こったのか。ホー・チ・ミンはコミュニストの手先なのか、それとも救国の士なのか。その両方なのか、そのどちらでもないのか。ジュネーヴ協定はどうなるのか。SEATOと冷戦はどうなるのか。ドミノ理論はどうなるのか。そういう問題やその他無数の問題についてアメリカの世論は分裂してしまった。上院議会から街角にいたるまで、激しい論争が繰り広げられた。そしてピンストライプの背広に身を包んだエリート連中も、もっとも基本的な政治的事項においてさえ見解をまとめることができなかった。その夏確かだったことは、人々

and still is, that you don't make war without knowing why. Knowledge, of course, is always imperfect, but it seemed to me that when a nation goes to war it must have reasonable confidence in the justice and ❶imperative of its cause. You can't ❷fix your mistakes. Once people are dead, you can't make them undead.

🎧**A04**

In any case those were my convictions, and back in college I had taken a modest stand against the war. Nothing radical, no ❸hothead stuff, just ringing a few doorbells for ❹Gene McCarthy, ❺composing a few tedious, uninspired editorials for the campus newspaper. Oddly, though, it was almost entirely an intellectual activity. I brought some energy to it, of course, but it was the energy that accompanies almost any ❻abstract endeavor; I felt no personal danger; I felt no sense of an ❼impending crisis in my life. Stupidly, ❽with a kind of smug removal that I can't begin to fathom, I assumed that the problems of killing and dying did not fall within my special province.

🎧**A05**

The draft notice arrived on June 17, 1968. It was a humid afternoon, I remember, cloudy, very quiet, and I'd just come in from a round of golf. My mother and father were having lunch out in the

---

❽dominoes: ドミノ理論　★ある国の政体変更が、ドミノ倒しのように近隣諸国の政体変更につながるとする外交政策の考え方。アメリカによるヴェトナム戦争参戦の際にこの理論が用いられた。❾in pinstripes: ピンストライプ・スーツを着た　★実業・政治界のエリートというイメージ。［以上014〜015ページ脚注］❶imperative: 回避しようのない要請　❷fix: 直す　❸hothead stuff: 過激な言動　❹Gene McCarthy: ジーン・マッカーシー　★Eugene McCarthy。リンドン・ジョンソン大統領のヴェトナム介入政策への批判者として知られた。　❺composing a few tedious,

が精神的に混乱しているという事実だけであった。理由もわからずに戦争なんかできない、というのがそのときの私の意見だったし、その意見は今でも変わらない。もちろん本当に何かをわかるなんてことは不可能である。しかしいやしくもひとつの国家が戦争に向かうときには、国家は自らの正義に対するしかるべき確信を持ち、揺るがざる根拠を持つべきである。間違っていたからあとで修復しますというわけにはいかないのだ。一度死んでしまった人間は、どれだけ手を尽くしても生き返りはしないのだから。

　何はともあれそれが私の信念だった。当時大学で私は穏健な反戦的立場をとっていた。全然ラディカルじゃないし、性急な意見にも飛びつかなかった。ジーン・マッカーシーのために戸別訪問みたいなことをちょっとやったり、凡庸にして退屈な論説を大学新聞のためにいくつか書いたりしただけだった。でも奇妙と言えば奇妙なのだが、私にとってそれは純粋な知的作業だった。私はけっこう夢中になってとりくんだのだが、しかしそれはどのような抽象的傾注にも見受けられるエネルギーであった。私は自分の身が危険にさらされるなんて思ってもみなかったのだ。自らの人生の岐路がすぐそこに迫っていることにも思いいたらなかったのだ。お気楽にも、どうしてそんなことを思ったのか自分でも見当がつかないのだが、適当にいろんなことがうまくいって、殺したり殺されたりといった問題は自分の身にだけは降りかかってこないものと決めこんでいたのだ。

　徴兵通知は1968年の六月十七日に舞い込んだ。蒸し暑い午後だったことを覚えている。曇っていて、とても静かだった。私はゴルフを一ラウンドやって帰ってきたところだった。母と父はキッチンで昼食をとっ

uninspired editorials for the campus newspaper: 凡庸にして退屈な論説を大学新聞のためにいくつか書いたりしただけだった★tediousは「退屈な」、uninspiredは「独創性のない」。　❻abstract endeavor: 抽象的努力❼impending: 差し迫った　❽with a kind of smug removal that I can't begin to fathom: いまとなってはおよそ理解できない、ある種のうぬぼれたへだたりをもって　★smugは「独りよがりの」、can't begin to ...は「とうてい〜できない」、fathomは「〜を理解する」。

kitchen. I remember opening up the letter, scanning the first few lines, feeling the blood go thick behind my eyes. I remember a sound in my head. It wasn't thinking, just a silent howl. A million things all at once—I was too *good* for this war. Too smart, too ❶compassionate, too everything. It couldn't happen. I was ❷above it. ❸I had the world dicked—❹Phi Beta Kappa, ❺summa cum laude and president of the student body and ❻a full-ride scholarship for grad studies at Harvard. A mistake, maybe—a ❼foul-up in the paperwork. I was no soldier. I hated Boy Scouts. I hated camping out. I hated dirt and tents and mosquitoes. The sight of blood made me ❽queasy, I couldn't tolerate authority, and I didn't know a rifle from a ❾slingshot. I was a *liberal*, for Christ sake: If they needed fresh bodies, why not draft some back-to-the-stone-age ❿hawk? Or ⓫some dumb jingo in his hard hat and Bomb Hanoi button, or one of ⓬LBJ's pretty daughters, or ⓭Westmoreland's whole handsome family—nephews and nieces and baby grandson. There should be a law, I thought. If you support a war, if you think it's worth the price, that's fine, but you have to ⓮put your own precious fluids on the line. You have to head for the front and ⓯hook up with an infantry unit and help spill the blood. And you have to

---

❶compassionate: 心優しい、思いやりのある　❷above: (〜には) 良すぎる　❸I had the world dicked: 俺は世界を丸め込んでいた　★dickは「〜をだます、欺く」。❹Phi Beta Kappa: ファイ・ベータ・カッパ、優等大学生友愛会の会員　❺summa cum laude: 最優等で　❻a full-ride scholarship for grad studies at Harvard: ハーヴァード大学の大学院の特待生奨学金　★full-rideは俗語で「費用が全額支払われる」。❼foul-up: ヘマ、ポカ　★インフォーマルな語。❽queasy: 吐きけがする、むかむかする　❾slingshot: (ゴムで飛ばすY字型の) パチンコ　❿hawk: タカ派

ていた。封筒を開けて、最初の数行にさっと目を通したところで、目の奥のあたりで血液が急にどろりと重くなったことを覚えている。頭の中でそのときに聞こえた音を私は覚えている。それは思考ではなかった。それは声にならない嗚咽だった。まさに青天の霹靂だった。なんで俺のような立派な人間がこんな戦争に行かなくちゃならないんだ。頭だっていいし、心優しいし、その他何をとっても優秀だ。こんなことあってたまるものか。俺はそんなことにかかずらわっているような人間じゃないんだ。俺は世界を手に入れたんだ —— ファイ・ベータ・カッパ、最優等卒業、生徒会長、ハーヴァード大学の大学院の特待生奨学金。何かの間違いかもしれない。事務処理に手違いがあったのだ。俺は兵隊向きの人間じゃない。ボーイ・スカウトだって嫌いだったのだ。キャンプするのだって嫌だった。泥やらテントやら蚊やら、そういうものが嫌いだった。血を見るだけで気分が悪くなったし、権威というものに我慢ができない。ライフル銃とパチンコの違いさえわからないのだ。それに私はなんといってもリベラルだったのだ。新兵が必要なのなら、どうして「ヴェトナムを石器時代に戻せ」と叫ぶようなタカ派のやつらを徴兵しないんだ。あるいは作業ヘルメットをかぶって「ハノイ爆撃」というバッジをつけたどこかの間抜けの戦争支持者を。あるいはジョンソン大統領の可愛い三人娘の一人を。あるいはウェストモーランドの一家全員（甥から姪から幼い孫にいたるまで）を。法律でそう決めるべきだ、と私は思った。もし誰かが戦争を支持するのなら、それが代償を払うに値すると思うのならそれでもけっこう。しかしそういう人間は自分の命をかけて前線に出ていただきたい。そういう人間は前線に行って、歩兵部隊の仲間入りをして、どうぞ血を流していただきたい。そしてそこに自分の

⓫some dumb jingo: どこかの間抜けの戦争支持者　⓬LBJ: リンドン・ジョンソン（第36代米国大統領 [1963-69]）　★Lyndon Baines Johnson。ケネディ暗殺後に政権を継いだ大統領で、ヴェトナム戦争を拡大し、国内での支持を失う。　⓭Westmoreland:（ウィリアム・チャイルズ・）ウェストモーランド　★William Childs Westmoreland。ヴェトナム戦争でアメリカ軍の指揮を執った。
⓮put your own precious fluids on the line:　★直訳すれば「自分の大切な体液を前線に出す」。
⓯hook up with an infantry unit: 歩兵部隊（an infantry unit）の仲間入りをする

bring along your wife, or your kids, or your lover. A *law*, I thought.

🎧**A06**

I remember the rage in my stomach. Later it burned down to a
❶smoldering self-pity, then to numbness. At dinner that night my
father asked what my plans were. "Nothing," I said. "Wait."

🎧**A07**

I spent the summer of 1968 working in an Armour meatpacking
plant in my hometown of Worthington, Minnesota. The plant spe-
cialized in pork products, and for eight hours a day I stood on ❷a
quarter-mile assembly line—more properly, a disassembly line—re-
moving ❸blood clots from the necks of dead pigs. My job title, I
believe, was Declotter. After slaughter, ❹the hogs were decapitated,
❺split down the length of the belly, ❻pried open, ❼eviscerated, and
❽strung up by the hind hocks on a high conveyer belt. ❾Then gravity took over. By the time a ❿carcass reached my spot on the line,
the fluids had mostly ⓫drained out, everything except for thick
clots of blood in the neck and ⓬upper chest cavity. To remove the
stuff, I used a kind of water gun. The machine was heavy, maybe
eighty pounds, and was suspended from the ceiling by a heavy rubber cord. There was some bounce to it, ⓭an elastic up-and-down
give, and the trick was to ⓮maneuver the gun with your whole
body, not lifting with the arms, just letting the rubber cord do the
work for you. At one end was a trigger; ⓯at the muzzle end was a

---

❶smoldering:（火・焼け跡などが）くすぶっている　❷a quarter-mile assembly line: 四〇〇メー
トルに及ぶベルト・コンベア　★an assembly lineは「組立ライン、流れ作業」。❸blood clots: 血
の塊　❹the hogs were decapitated: 豚は頭を切断され　★hogは「（成長した食肉用の）豚」、
decapitateは「～の頭部を切断する」。❺split down the length of the belly: 腹を縦に裂かれ
★down the length of . . .は「～の端から端まで」。❻pried open: 大きく開かれ　★pry . . . open
は「～を力ずくで開ける」。❼eviscerate(d): ～から内臓を取り出す❽strung up by the hind

奥さんなり自分の子供なり自分の恋人なりを一緒に連れて行っていただきたい。そういう法律があってしかるべきだと私は思った。

　私は自分の腹の中に湧き起こってきた怒りを覚えている。やがてその炎は収まり、ぶすぶすと燻って自己憐憫になった。それから無感覚がやってきた。夕食の席で父が私に尋ねた。どうするつもりなんだと。「わからない」と私は言った。「待って」

　1968年の夏、私は我が故郷であるミネソタ州ワージントンにあるアーマー畜肉工場で働いていた。その工場は豚肉処理を専門にしていた。そして一日に八時間、私は四〇〇メートルに及ぶベルト・コンベアの前に立っていた。もっともこのベルト・コンベアは組立ではなくバラすことを目的にしていた。そこで私は死んだ豚の首から血の塊を取り去った。私の職掌名は血糊取りだった。そうだったと思う。畜殺されたあとで、豚は頭を切断され、腹を縦に裂かれ、大きく開かれ、内臓を抜かれ、丈の高いベルト・コンベアに後ろ脚から吊るされる。あとは引力が仕事をしてくれる。その死体が私のところにまわってくる頃には、死体の体液はほとんど全部抜けてしまっている。首と胸の上の方にある穴にぶよっとした血の塊が残っているだけだ。それを取り除くために、私はウォーター・ガンのようなものを使った。重い機械だった。三十五キロくらいあったと思うが、それが天井から頑丈なゴムのコードで吊り下げられていた。それには多少弾みがついていた。上下にひょいひょいと揺れるのだ。ガンを扱うコツは体ぜんたいを使うことである。両腕だけで持ち上げようとしたりしてはいけない。ゴムのコードの力をうまく利用すればいいのだ。片方の端が引き金になっている。砲口の側には小さ

hocks: 後ろ脚 (the hind hocks) から吊るされて　★string . . . upは「〜を（一列に）吊るす」。
❾ Then gravity took over: ★直訳すると「それから重力が（その仕事を）引き継いだ」。❿ carcass: （動物の）死体、死骸 ⓫ drained out: 抜けてしまっている ⓬ upper chest cavity: 胸の上の方にある穴　★cavityは「穴、腔」。⓭ an elastic up-and-down give: ★直訳は「上下に伸び縮みする弾力性」。⓮ maneuver: （人・物）を巧みに動かす ⓯ at the muzzle end: 砲口の側には

small nozzle and a steel roller brush. As a carcass passed by, you'd lean forward and swing the gun up against the clots and squeeze the trigger, all in one motion, and the brush would ❶whirl and water would come shooting out and you'd hear a quick splattering sound as the clots dissolved into a fine red mist. It was not pleasant work. Goggles were a necessity, and a rubber apron, but even so it was like standing for eight hours a day under ❷a lukewarm blood-shower. At night I'd go home smelling of pig. It wouldn't go away. Even after a hot bath, scrubbing hard, the stink was always there—like old bacon, or sausage, a dense greasy pig-stink that soaked deep into my skin and hair. Among other things, I remember, ❸it was tough getting dates that summer. I felt isolated; I spent a lot of time alone. And there was also that draft notice ❹tucked away in my wallet.

🎧A08

In the evenings I'd sometimes borrow my father's car and drive aimlessly around town, feeling sorry for myself, thinking about the war and the pig factory and how my life seemed to ❺be collapsing toward slaughter. I felt paralyzed. All around me the options seemed to be narrowing, ❻as if I were hurtling down a huge black funnel, the whole world ❼squeezing in tight. There was no happy way out. The government had ended most graduate school ❽deferments; the waiting lists for the National Guard and Reserves were impossibly long; my health was solid; ❾I didn't qualify for CO sta-

---

❶whirl: ぐるぐると回転する　❷a lukewarm bloodshower: 生温かい血のシャワー　❸it was tough getting dates: デートの相手をみつけるのが大変だった　❹tucked away in . . .: ～にしまいこまれて　❺be collapsing toward slaughter: ★直訳は「潰滅へと向かって崩壊していく」。 ❻as if I were hurtling down a huge black funnel: 巨大な暗い漏斗を落下していくような感じだった　★hurtle down . . .は「～を猛烈な速さで落ちる」。　❼squeezing in: 無理矢理迫ってくる ❽deferments: 徴兵猶予　❾I didn't qualify for CO status: 良心的戦闘忌避者になる資格はなかっ

なノズルと鉄のローラー・ブラシがついている。死体が前を通り過ぎていくと、体を前にかがめて銃口を血の塊につけるようにして、引き金を引く。それを一回の動作でやる。するとブラシがぐるぐると回転し、水が勢いよく噴き出す。そして血の塊が細かな赤い霧へと分解していくぴちぴちっという短い音が聞こえる。それは決して心楽しい仕事ではなかった。ゴーグルは必需品だった。ゴムのエプロンも。でもそういう格好をしたところでやはり、私としては一日に八時間生温かい血のシャワーを浴びているような気分だった。夜になると、私は豚の匂いを体につけたまま家に帰った。どれだけ洗っても匂いは落ちなかった。熱い風呂に入って体をごしごしとこすったあとでさえ、臭みはまだそこに残っていた。古いベーコンみたいに、ソーセージみたいに、べっとりとした脂っぽい豚の匂いが皮膚と髪のずっと奥にまで染みついてしまったのだ。そのうえ、私はその夏、デートする女の子をうまくみつけることができなかった。私は孤独だった。私は多くの時間をひとりぼっちで過ごした。おまけに私の財布の中には徴兵通知がしまいこまれていた。

日が暮れると私はときどき父の車を借りて、あてもなく街を走らせた。運転しながら惨めな気持ちになった。戦争と豚肉工場のことを思った。そして自分の人生がどうしようもなく落ちぶれていくように思えた。身動きがとれなくなり、私のまわりの選択肢がどんどん狭まっていくみたいだった。巨大な暗い漏斗を落下していくような感じだった。世界中がぎゅっと固く締まっていくのだ。幸せな出口なんてそこにはない。政府は大学院生に対する徴兵猶予をほとんど全面的に中止してしまった。州軍と予備役への申込みリストは気が遠くなるくらい長大なものになっていた。私の健康はもうしぶんなかった。良心的戦闘忌避者に

た　★CO=conscientious objector

tus—no religious grounds, no history as a pacifist. Moreover, I could not claim to be opposed to war as a matter of general principle. There were occasions, I believed, when a nation was justified in using military force to achieve its ends, to stop a Hitler or some comparable evil, and I told myself that in such circumstances I would've willingly marched off to the battle. The problem, though, was that a draft board did not let you choose your war.

🎧**A09**

Beyond all this, or at the very center, was the raw fact of terror. I did not want to die. ❶Not ever. But certainly not then, not there, not in a wrong war. Driving up Main Street, past the courthouse and ❷the Ben Franklin store, I sometimes felt the fear spreading inside me like weeds. I imagined myself dead. I imagined myself doing things I could not do—charging an enemy position, taking aim at another human being.

🎧**A10**

At some point in mid-July I began thinking seriously about Canada. The border lay a few hundred miles north, an eight-hour drive. Both my conscience and my instincts were telling me to ❸make a break for it, just take off and run like hell and never stop. In the beginning the idea seemed purely abstract, the word Canada printing itself out in my head; but after a time I could see particular shapes and images, the sorry details of my own future—a hotel room in Winnipeg, a ❹battered old suitcase, my father's eyes as I

---

❶ Not ever.: ★neverとほぼ同意だが次のnot thenにつながるようこう書かれている。　❷the Ben Franklin store: ★多種雑多な商品を扱う全米規模のチェーン店。　❸make a break for it: ★直訳は「あそこめざして走り出せ」。　❹battered: ぼろぼろの

なる資格はなかった。しかるべき宗教的背景もなかったし、平和主義者としての経歴もなかった。そのうえ、私は原則としてどのような戦争も一切認めないと主張することはできなかった。時には国が目的を達するために軍隊を使用せざるを得ない場合だってあると私は信じていた。たとえばヒットラーや、あるいはそれに匹敵する悪をおしとどめるために。そういう状況であれば自分だって進んで戦場に出向くさと私は思っていた。問題は徴兵委員会がこちらに戦争を選ばせてくれないことである。

　これら一切を超えて、あるいはこれら一切のまさに中心に存在したのは、恐怖という動かしがたい事実だった。私は死にたくなかった。それは言うまでもないことだ。でも私としてはよりによって今、あんなところで、誤った戦争の中で死にたくなかった。メイン・ストリートに沿って車を走らせ、裁判所の建物とベン・フランクリン・ストアの前を通り過ぎながら、時折私は自分の体の中に恐怖が雑草のようにはびこっていくのを感じた。私は自分が死んでいるところを想像した。私は自分ができるはずのないことをやっているところを想像した。敵の陣地を攻撃したり、他の人間を銃で狙ったりしているところを。

　七月の中頃になって、私はカナダ行きのことを真剣に考慮するようになっていた。北に数百マイル行けば、そこはもう国境だった。車なら八時間で着く。私の良心も私の本能も、思い切ってそうしろと告げていた。荷物をまとめてさっさとトンズラしちゃうのだ。最初のうち、それはまったくの抽象的な考えにすぎなかった。カナダという文字が頭の中にただ印刷されているだけだった。でもほどなく具体的な形や輪郭が見えてきた。私の哀れな未来の詳細。ウィニペグのホテルの部屋、すりき

tried to explain myself over the telephone. I could almost hear his voice, and my mother's. Run, I'd think. Then I'd think, Impossible. Then a second later I'd think, *Run.*

∩A11

It was a kind of ❶schizophrenia. A moral split. I couldn't make up my mind. I feared the war, yes, but I also feared ❷exile. I was afraid of walking away from my own life, my friends and my family, my whole history, everything that mattered to me. I feared losing the respect of my parents. I feared the law. ❸I feared ridicule and censure. My hometown was a conservative little spot on the prairie, a place where tradition ❹counted, and it was easy to imagine people sitting around a table down at the old Gobbler Café on Main Street, ❺coffee cups poised, the conversation slowly ❻zeroing in on the young O'Brien kid, how the ❼damned sissy had taken off for Canada. At night, when I couldn't sleep, I'd sometimes carry on fierce arguments with those people. I'd be screaming at them, telling them ❽how much I detested their blind, thoughtless, automatic ❾acquiescence to it all, their simpleminded patriotism, their prideful ignorance, ❿their love-it-or-leave-it platitudes, how they were sending me off to fight a war they didn't understand and didn't want to understand. ⓫I held them responsible. By God, yes, I *did.* All of them—I held them personally and individually responsible— ⓬the polyestered Kiwanis boys, the merchants and farmers, the pi-

---

❶schizophrenia: 統合失調症 ❷exile: 追放者の身の上 ❸I feared ridicule and censure: 私はあざけりや非難を恐れた❹count(ed): 意味を持つ、物を言う ❺coffee cups poised: コーヒーカップを手に ★poiseは「～をかまえる、～を上にたもつ」。 ❻zero(ing) in on . . .: ～にだんだん収斂していく ❼damned sissy: 情けないくじなし ❽how much I detested . . .: ～に僕がいかにうんざりしているか★detestは「～を忌み嫌う」。 ❾acquiescence: 追従、黙従 ★フォーマルな語。
❿their love-it-or-leave-it platitudes: ★"take it or leave it"〈受け入れるか、拒むか、どっちかに

れたスーツケース、私が電話で事情を説明しているときの父の目つき。私は彼の声を想像することもできた。そして母の声も。逃げるんだ、と私は思った。そして思い返した。いや、そんなこと不可能だと。そしてその一秒後にまた私は思うのだった。逃げるんだ、と。

それは一種の分裂症だった。心が二つに割れてしまったのだ。決心がつかなかった。戦争は怖い。でも国外に逃げることもやはり怖かった。私は私自身の人生や、私の家族や友人たちや、私の経歴や、そういう私にとって意味のある何もかもを捨てていくということが怖かった。私は両親にがっかりされることを恐れた。私は法律を恐れた。私はあざけられたり、非難されたりすることを恐れた。私が生まれたのは大平原の中にある保守的な小さな町だった。そこでは伝統というものが重んじられていた。きっと人々はお馴染みのゴブラー・カフェのテーブルを囲んで、コーヒーカップを手に、口を開けばオブライエンの息子のことを話題にするのだろう。あの腰抜け息子は尻に帆たてててカナダに逃げたんだぞ、と。眠れない夜には、私はときどきそういう連中と激しい議論を交わしたものだった。私は彼らに向かって怒鳴った。盲目的に、何も考えずに、与えられたものに黙ってただ追従するようなあんたたちのやりかたに、僕はもううんざりしているんだ。単細胞の愛国心にも、自信満々の無知さ加減にも、「国を愛する者は国に従え、文句は言うな」式の陳腐な標語にも、つくづくうんざりしているのだと。だいたい自分たちには理解できないし、理解したいとも思わないような戦争に、どうしてあんたたちは僕を送り出そうとしているんだ。責任はあんたたちにあるんだぞ、と私は指弾した。そう、私は本気で彼らを指弾したのだ。あんたたち全員、その一人ひとりに責任があるんだぞと。キワーニス・クラブに

しろ）という決まり文句の変形。⓫I held them responsible: 責任はあんたたちにあるんだぞ、と私は指弾した　★hold ... responsibleは「（人）の責任にする」。⓬the polyestered Kiwanis boys: キワーニス・クラブに入っているエリートたち　★polyesteredは「安っぽく小ぎれいな」、Kiwanisは「（商標）キワーニス・クラブ」でアメリカの実業家が組織する地域奉仕団体。

ous churchgoers, the chatty housewives, the PTA and the Lions club and the Veterans of Foreign Wars and ❶the fine upstanding gentry out at the country club. ❷They didn't know Bao Dai from the man in the moon. They didn't know history. They didn't know the first thing about ❸Diem's tyranny, or the nature of Vietnamese nationalism, or the long colonialism of the French—this was all too damned complicated, it required some reading—but no matter, it was a war to stop the Communists, plain and simple, which was how they liked things, and you were ❹a treasonous pussy if you had second thoughts about killing or dying for plain and simple reasons.

🎧A12

I was ❺bitter, sure. But it was so much more than that. The emotions went from outrage to terror to bewilderment to guilt to sorrow and then back again to outrage. I felt a sickness inside me. Real disease.

🎧A13

Most of this I've told before, or at least hinted at, but what I have never told is the full truth. ❻How I cracked. How at work one morning, standing on the pig line, I felt something break open in my chest. I don't know what it was. I'll never know. But it was real, ❼I know that much, it was ❽a physical rupture—a cracking-leak-

---

❶the fine upstanding gentry out at the country club: カントリー・クラブに出入りするお上品な紳士たち　★fineは「ご立派な」、upstandingは「清廉潔白な」、gentryはやや古い語で「上流階級の人たち」。　❷They didn't know Bao Dai from the man in the moon: 彼らにはバオダイと月世界人の違いだってわかりはしないのだ　★Bao Daiはヴェトナムのグエン朝第13代皇帝。1954年のジュネーブ協定後に南ヴェトナム元首となったが、55年アメリカの支援を受けた新首相ゴディンジエム（事項❸参照）に国民投票で敗れてパリに亡命した。　❸Diem's tyranny: ★ジエムはヴェト

入っているエリートたちや、商人たちや農民たちや、敬虔なキリスト信者たちや、おしゃべりな奥さんたち、PTA、ライオンズ・クラブ、海外派遣軍人会、そしてカントリー・クラブに出入りするお上品な紳士たち。彼らにはバオダイと月世界人の違いだってわかりはしないのだ。彼らには歴史なんてわかりはしない。ジエムがどんな独裁制を敷いていたか、ヴェトナムのナショナリズムがどのようなものか、あるいは長いフランスによる植民地統治についてなんてこれっぽっちも知らない。そういう事情は非常に複雑だし、それを理解するには本を読んで研究しなくてはならない。しかしそんなことは彼らにはどうだっていいのだ。それはコミュニストを封じ込めるための戦争なのだ。単純明快である。そしてそれがまさに彼らの求めているものなのだ。そしてそういうシンプルな大義のために人を殺したり殺されたりすることにちょっとでも疑いをもったら、弱虫の裏切り者ということになってしまうのだ。

　確かに私は頭に来ていた。でもそれだけではなかった。感情は憤怒から恐怖にかわり、困惑から罪悪感にかわり、悲しみにかわり、そしてまた憤怒に戻った。体がおかしくなってしまったようだった。これはもうまさに病だった。

　こういうことの多くの部分を私は以前に書いた。あるいは少なくともそれとなく匂わせた。でも私はその真実の全貌をきちんと書いたことはない。私がどのようにして潰れてしまったかについて。ある朝仕事場に行って、食肉処理のラインの前に立っているときに、私は自分の胸の中で何かがばりっと折れて開いてしまったのを感じた。それが何であるのかはわからなかった。この先もわからないと思う。しかしそれは間違えようのない事実だった。私にはそれがわかった。それは肉体的破断だっ

ナム戦争時、アメリカの支援に依存して北ヴェトナムの共産政権と抗争を続けた。1963年仏教徒弾圧事件を機に起きたクーデターで暗殺された。　❹a treasonous pussy: 裏切り者の弱虫　★treasonous（=treasonable）は「反逆罪に値する」、pussyは「（男の）弱虫、意気地なし」。❺bitter: 慣っている　❻How I cracked: 私がどのようにして参ってしまったか　★crackは「（疲労・恐怖・緊張などで）耐えきれなくなる」。❼I know that much: そこまではわかる　❽a physical rupture: 肉体的破裂

ing-popping feeling. I remember dropping my water gun. Quickly, almost without thought, I took off my apron and walked out of the plant and drove home. It was midmorning, I remember, and the house was empty. Down in my chest there was still that leaking sensation, something very warm and precious spilling out, and I was covered with blood and hog-stink, and for a long while I just concentrated on holding myself together. I remember taking a hot shower. I remember packing a suitcase and carrying it out to the kitchen, standing very still for a few minutes, looking carefully at the familiar objects all around me. The old chrome toaster, the telephone, the pink and white ❶Formica on the kitchen counters. The room was full of bright sunshine. Everything sparkled. My house, I thought. My life. I'm not sure how long I stood there, but later I ❷scribbled out a short note to my parents.

What it said, exactly, I don't recall now. Something vague. Taking off, will call, love Tim.

🎧A14

I drove north.

It's a ❸blur now, as it was then, and all I remember is ❹a sense of high velocity and the feel of the steering wheel in my hands. I was riding on adrenaline. A giddy feeling, in a way, except there was the dreamy edge of impossibility to it—like running a dead-end

---

❶Formica:（商標）フォーマイカ　★家具などに使用される耐熱性の合成樹脂板。　❷scribbled out ...:〜を走り書きした　❸blur: ぼんやり［かすんで］見えるもの　❹a sense of high velocity: ★直訳すると「高速度の感覚」。

た。何かがばりっと折れたような、何かが漏出しているような、何かが
ぽんと弾けたような、そういう感触だったのだ。ウォーター・ガンを下
に落としたのを覚えている。即座に、ほとんど何も考えずに、私はエプ
ロンを取り、工場を出て、車で家に帰った。昼前で、家の中ががらんと
していたことを記憶している。私の胸の中にはまださっきの漏洩感が
残っていた。何か温かく貴重なものが体の中で漏れ出ていた。そして私
は血と豚の匂いに覆われていた。私は自分がばらばらになってしまわな
いように、長いあいだじっと神経を集中していた。熱いシャワーに入っ
たことを記憶している。私はスーツケースに荷物を詰めて、キッチンに
それを運んだ。そしてそこに立ちすくんだまま、まわりにある見慣れた
事物を注意深く眺めていた。古いクロームのトースター、電話機、キッ
チン・カウンターの上のピンクと白の合成樹脂パネル。部屋は明るい陽
光に満ちていた。何もかもがぴかぴかに光っていた。僕の家、と私は
思った。僕の生活。どれくらい長くそこに立っていたのか、私にはわか
らない。でもそのあとで私は両親に向けて短い書き置きを書いた。

　どんなことを書いたか、正確には思い出せない。どうとでも取れるよ
うなことだったと思う。ちょっと旅に出る、連絡する、ティムより。

　私は北に向けて車を走らせた。
　今ではすべてがぼやけている。でもそのときだってやはり同じように
ぼやけていたのだ。覚えているのは速度の速さと、両手の中にあるハン
ドルの感触だけだ。私はアドレナリンに浮かされていた。くらくらする
ような気分、というところ。でもそこには果たされることのない夢の気
配があった。出口なき袋小路の迷路を走っているような感じだ。ハッ

maze—no way out—it couldn't come to a happy conclusion and yet I was doing it anyway because it was all I could think of to do. It was pure flight, fast and mindless. I had no plan. Just hit the border at high speed and crash through and keep on running. Near dusk I passed through Bemidji, then turned northeast toward International Falls. I spent the night in the car behind a closed-down gas station a half mile from the border. In the morning, after gassing up, I headed straight west along the Rainy River, which separates Minnesota from Canada, and which for me separated one life from another. The land was mostly wilderness. Here and there I passed a motel or bait shop, but otherwise ❶the country unfolded in great sweeps of pine and birch and sumac. Though it was still August, the air already had the smell of October, football season, piles of yellow-red leaves, everything crisp and clean. I remember a huge blue sky. Off to my right was the Rainy River, wide as a lake in places, and beyond the Rainy River was Canada.

🎧A15

For a while I just drove, not aiming at anything, then in the late morning I began looking for a place to lie low for a day or two. I was exhausted, and scared sick, and around noon ❷I pulled into an old fishing resort called the Tip Top Lodge. Actually it was not a lodge at all, just eight or nine tiny yellow cabins ❸clustered on a

---

❶the country unfolded in great sweeps of pine and birch and sumac: 大地は何にも邪魔されることなく、松や樺（birch）や漆（sumac）の木を見渡すかぎりどこまでも広げていた ★unfoldは「（折りたたんである紙・布など）を開く、展開する」、sweepは「（大地などの）広がり」。❷I pulled into an old fishing resort: ★直訳すれば「釣り客相手の古いホテルに車を入れた」。❸clustered on . . .: ～に集まった

ピーな結末に辿り着くことなんか不可能である。にもかかわらず、私にはそうするしかない。それ以外にどうすればいいのか思いつけないから。それはまるっきりの潰走だった。何も考えずに、さっさと逃げるだけ。私には計画というものがなかった。ハイスピードで国境に着いて、それを突破し、そしてまた逃げつづける。夕方近くに私はベミジーを抜けた。そして進路を北東に転じ、インターナショナル・フォールズに向かった。夜は閉鎖されたガソリン・スタンドの裏手に車を停めて、その中で眠った。国境まであと半マイルの地点だった。夜が明けると、私は車に給油し、レイニー河に沿ってまっすぐ西に走った。レイニー河によってミネソタとカナダとは隔てられているわけだが、それはまた私のこれまでの人生ともうひとつの人生を隔ててもいた。まわりの土地にはほとんど人の気配はなかった。ときどきモーテルや釣り餌店がぽつんぽつんと目についたが、それを別にすれば大地は何に邪魔されることもなく、松や樺や漆の木を見渡すかぎりどこまでも展開させていた。まだ八月だったけれど、あたりにはもう十月の匂いが感じられた。フットボールのシーズン、紅葉した樹木、きりっと澄んだ空気。私は高く青い空を思い出す。私の右手にはレイニー河が流れていた。ところどころでまるで湖のように河幅が広くなっていた。そしてそのレイニー河の対岸はもうカナダだった。

　しばらくのあいだ、私はあてもなく車を走らせた。昼近くになって、私は一日二日ゆっくり体を休められそうなところを探し始めた。私は消耗して、脅えきっていた。昼頃に私はティップトップ・ロッジという名の古い釣り客相手のホテルをみつけた。でも実際にはそれはどう見てもロッジというような代物ではなかった。八軒か九軒の黄色い小屋<ruby>小屋<rt>コッテージ</rt></ruby>が北に

peninsula that **❶**jutted northward into the Rainy River. The place was in sorry shape. There was a dangerous wooden dock, an old **❷**minnow tank, a **❸**flimsy tar paper boathouse along the shore. The main building, which stood in a cluster of pines on high ground, seemed to lean heavily to one side, like a **❹**cripple, **❺**the roof sagging toward Canada. Briefly, I thought about turning around, just giving up, but then I got out of the car and walked up to the front porch.

🎧A16

The man who opened the door that day is the hero of my life. How do I say this without sounding **❻**sappy? **❼**Blurt it out—the man saved me. He offered exactly what I needed, without questions, without any words at all. He took me in. He was there at the critical time—a silent, watchful presence. Six days later, when it ended, I was unable to find a proper way to thank him, and I never have, and so, **❽**if nothing else, this story represents a small gesture of gratitude **❾**twenty years overdue.

🎧A17

Even after two decades I can close my eyes and return to that porch at the Tip Top Lodge. I can see the old guy staring at me. Elroy Berdahl: eighty-one years old, skinny and shrunken and mostly bald. He wore a flannel shirt and brown work pants. In one hand, I remember, he carried a green apple, a small paring knife in the oth-

---

❶jutted northward into the Rainy River: 北に向けてレイニー河に突き出した　★jut into ...は「～の中へ突き出る」。 **❷**minnow: ヒメハヤ、ミノウ（淡水小魚）　★釣り餌として用いられる。 **❸**flimsy: 薄っぺらな、べらべらした　**❹**cripple: ★足の不自由な人を指すときの蔑称。 **❺**the roof sagging toward Canada: 屋根がカナダの方向にかしいでいる　★分詞構文。sag toward ...は「～の方に傾く」。 **❻**sappy: =sentimental　**❼**Blurt it out: ★直訳は「思い切って言ってしまえ」。 **❽**if nothing else: 少なくとも　**❾**twenty years overdue: ★直訳は「二十年遅れた」。

向けてレイニー河に突き出した岬のような土地に集まっているだけだ。見るからに見すぼらしい場所だった。あぶなっかしそうな木製の桟橋があり、釣り餌用の小魚を入れた水槽があり、河のほとりにはぺらぺらしたタール紙を貼ったボート小屋が建っていた。少し小高くなった場所の、松の木立の中にある母屋は、ぐっと大きく片方に傾いているように見えた。まるで片脚が悪い人のように、屋根がカナダの方向にかしいでいるのだ。一瞬私はそのまま回れ右をして帰ってしまいそうになった。でも思い直して車を降り、母屋の玄関まで歩いていった。

　その日そのドアを開けた男は、私の生涯のヒーローである。やれやれ、いったいどういう言葉を使って表現すればその馬鹿馬鹿しさを回避することができるだろう？　あれこれ考えずに素直に言っちゃうのが一番だろうと思う。その人物が私の人生を救ってくれたのだ。彼は私の求めていたものをそっくりそのまま提供してくれた。何も質問せず、余計なことはただのひとことも言わず。彼は私を中に入れた。いちばん大事なときに、彼はそこにいたのだ —— 何も言わず、しっかりと気を配って。六日間かけてそれが終わったとき、どういう形で彼に感謝の意を表わせばいいのか私には見当もつかなかった。そして今にいたるまでわからない。そのままもう二十年が過ぎてしまった。しかし何はともあれ、この作品は彼に対する私のささやかな感謝のしるしである。

　二十年を経た今でも、私は目を閉じればあのティップトップ・ロッジのポーチに戻っていくことができる。その老人がじっと私の顔を見ているところを想像できる。エルロイ・バーダール、八十一歳、痩せてしぼんでいて、髪はほとんどない。フランネルのシャツを着て、茶色の作業用ズボンをはいていた。彼が片手に青いリンゴを持って、もう一方の手

er. His eyes had ❶the bluish gray color of a razor blade, the same polished shine, and as he peered up at me I felt a strange sharpness, almost painful, a cutting sensation, as if his gaze were somehow slicing me open. In part, no doubt, it was my own sense of guilt, but even so I'm absolutely certain that the old man took one look and went right to the heart of things—a kid in trouble. When I asked for a room, Elroy made a little clicking sound with his tongue. He nodded, led me out to one of the cabins, and dropped a key in my hand. I remember smiling at him. I also remember wishing I hadn't. The old man shook his head as if to tell me it wasn't worth the bother.

"Dinner at five-thirty," he said. "You eat fish?"

"Anything," I said.

Elroy grunted and said, "❷I'll bet."

∩A18

We spent six days together at the Tip Top Lodge. Just the two of us. Tourist season was over, and there were no boats on the river, and the wilderness seemed to withdraw into a great permanent stillness. Over those six days Elroy Berdahl and I took most of our meals together. In the mornings we sometimes went out on long hikes into the woods, and at night we played Scrabble or listened

---

❶the bluish gray color of a razor blade: ★直訳は「かみそりの刃が持っている青みがかったグレー色」。 ❷I'll bet: (相手の発言に理解を示して) そうだろうね

に小さな果物ナイフを持っていたことを私は覚えている。彼の目の色は
アルミニウムのような青みを帯びたグレーだった。そして同じように艶
のある輝きを持っていた。私をじっと見つめるその目に、私は奇妙な
シャープさを感じた。痛みを感じたと言ってもいいくらいだった。まる
でその視線が私の体を切り裂いたみたいだった。もちろん私の罪悪感の
ようなものも作用していたのだと思う。でもそれはそれとしても、私は
絶対の確信を持ってこう思う。その老人は一目で物事の核心を理解した
のだ。この若者は悩みを抱えている、ということを。部屋はありますか
と私が尋ねると、エルロイは舌先でコンという小さな音を立てた。彼は
肯いて、私をキャビンのひとつに案内した。そして私の手に鍵を渡し
た。私は自分が彼ににっこりと微笑んだのを覚えている。そんなことし
なきゃよかったのにと後悔したことも。老人は頭を振った。わざわざそ
んなことしなくったっていいんだというように。

　「夕食は五時半だよ」と彼は言った。「あんた魚は食べるかね？」

　「なんだっていいです」と私は言った。

　エルロイはもそもそっと唸って、「まあそうだろうな」と言った。

　我々は六日間ティップトップ・ロッジで共に過ごした。我々二人きり
でだ。観光シーズンはもう終わっていたし、河には船は一隻も浮かんで
いなかった。まわりの原野は大いなる悠久の静寂の中に戻ってしまいそ
うに見えた。その六日のあいだずっと、エルロイ・バーダールと私はほ
とんどの食事を二人で一緒に食べた。午前中にときどき、我々は一緒に
森の中に長いハイキングに行った。夜には彼の大きな石造りの暖炉の前
でスクラブル・ゲームをやったり、レコードを聴いたり、本を読んだり

to records or sat reading in front of his big stone fireplace. At times I felt the awkwardness of an intruder, but Elroy accepted me into his quiet routine without fuss or ceremony. He took my presence for granted, the same way he might've sheltered a stray cat—no wasted sighs or pity—and there was never any talk about it. Just the opposite. What I remember more than anything is ❶the man's willful, almost ferocious silence. In all that time together, all those hours, he never asked the obvious questions: Why was I there? Why alone? Why so ❷preoccupied? If Elroy was curious about any of this, he was careful never to put it into words.

∩A19

My ❸hunch, though, is that he already knew. At least the basics. After all, it was 1968, and guys were burning draft cards, and Canada was just a boat ride away. Elroy Berdahl was no ❹hick. His bedroom, I remember, was cluttered with books and newspapers. He killed me at the Scrabble board, barely concentrating, and on those occasions when speech was necessary he had a way of compressing large thoughts into ❺small, cryptic packets of language. One evening, just at sunset, he pointed up at an owl circling over the violet-lighted forest to the west.

∩A20

"Hey, O'Brien," he said. "There's Jesus."

The man was sharp—he didn't miss much. Those razor eyes.

---

❶the man's willful, almost ferocious silence: その男の、激しいと言ってもいいくらいの（almost ferocious）きっぱりとした（willful）沈黙　❷preoccupied: 何かに心を奪われた様子の　❸hunch: 勘　❹hick:（侮蔑的に）田舎者　❺small, cryptic packets of language: 小さな、箴言めいたひとまとまりの言葉

した。時には私はなんだか自分が侵入者であるかのような居心地の悪さを感じた。しかしエルロイは彼の静かな日常生活の中に、何の混乱もなく何の儀式もなしに、私を受け入れてくれた。彼は私の存在を当たり前のこととして扱った。まるで野良猫の面倒でもみるみたいに。やれやれと溜め息をつくでもなく、妙に情をかけるでもなく。そしてそれについてとくに何かを言うわけでもなかった。それどころではない。私が何にもましてよく覚えているのは、その男の、激しいと言ってもいいくらいの、実にきっぱりとした沈黙なのだ。一緒にいるあいだ、始めから終わりまで、彼は私に対して、質問らしい質問は一切しなかった。どうしてここに来たのか？　どうして一人きりなのか？　どうしてそんなに考え込んでいるのか？　もし仮にエルロイがそれを知りたがっていたとしても、彼はそういうことは注意して口には出さないようにしていた。

　でも彼にはちゃんとわかっていたのだと思う。少なくともだいたいのところは。何といってもそれは1968年のことで、人々は徴兵カードを焼いていた。船で河を越えればそこはもうカナダだった。エルロイ・バーダールは無知無学な田舎者ではなかった。彼の居室に新聞や本がいっぱいに散らかっていたことを私は覚えている。彼はスクラブル・ゲームでいつも私を打ち負かした。ろくに身も入れずにだ。そして何かを言わなくてはならない場合には、彼は大きな思想を小さな簡潔な言葉にまとめて口にする術を心得ていた。ある夕暮れ、まさに太陽が没しようとしているときに、彼は西の方の、紫の光に染まった森の上空で円を描いているフクロウを指さした。

　「なあオブライエン」と彼は言った。「イエス様はいなさるぞ」

　その男はシャープだった。彼は細かいところまで見逃さなかった。そ

Now and then he'd catch me staring out at the river, at the far shore, and I could almost hear the ❶tumblers clicking in his head. Maybe I'm wrong, but I doubt it.

🎧A21

One thing for certain, he knew I was in desperate trouble. And he knew I couldn't talk about it. The wrong word—or even the right word—and I would've disappeared. ❷I was wired and jittery. My skin felt too tight. After supper one evening I vomited and went back to my cabin and lay down for a few moments and then vomited again; another time, in the middle of the afternoon, I began sweating and couldn't shut it off. I went through whole days ❸feeling dizzy with sorrow. I couldn't sleep; I couldn't lie still. At night I'd toss around in bed, half awake, half dreaming, imagining how I'd ❹sneak down to the beach and quietly push one of the old man's boats out into the river and start paddling my way toward Canada. There were times when I thought I'd ❺gone off the psychic edge. ❻I couldn't tell up from down, I was just falling, and late in the night I'd lie there ❼watching weird pictures spin through my head. Getting chased by the Border Patrol—helicopters and search-

---

❶tumblers: ★シリンダー錠の中の回転する金具。 ❷I was wired and jittery.: 私はぴりぴり、びくびくしていた ❸feel(ing) dizzy with sorrow: 悲しみのために頭がくらくらする❹sneak down to the beach: こっそりと河辺まで下りていって ❺gone off the psychic edge: ★go off the edgeで「崖から落ちてしまう＝気が変になる」の意の成句。 ❻I couldn't tell up from down: ★直訳すると「上と下の区別がつかなくなってしまった」。 ❼watching weird pictures spin through my head: ★直訳は「奇妙な画像が頭の中をくるくると回っていくのを見ながら」。

の剃刀のような目。時折彼は私が河を、そしてその対岸をじっと見つめているのに目をとめた。そして私には彼の頭の中で錠の中の金具が一回転するこちんという音を聞き取ることができるような気がした。あるいはそれは私の考えすぎかもしれない。でもたぶん間違っていないと思う。

　ひとつ確かなことがある。私がのっぴきならないトラブルを抱えこんでいることを彼は知っていたのだ。そして私がそれを他人に話すことができずにいるということも承知していた。確かに彼がひとことでも間違ったことを言ったら —— あるいはそのひとことが正しいことであったとしても —— 私はすぐにそこから姿を消しただろうと思う。私はそわそわ、びくびくしていた。皮膚が妙に突っ張っているように感じられた。ある夜の夕食のあとで私は食べたものをもどした。私は自分の小屋に帰って少し横になっていたが、またもどしてしまった。またある日の午後には、私はだらだらと汗をかきはじめた。そしていつまでたってもそれがとまらなかった。くる日もくる日も、朝から晩まで悲しみのために頭がくらくらするようだった。私は眠ることができなかった。じっと横になっていることができなかったのだ。私はベッドの中でばたばたと動きまわった。私は夢うつつに、自分がこっそりと河辺まで下りていって、老人の所有するボートのひとつをそっと河に押し出し、カナダに向けて漕ぎ出していく光景を想像した。自分の神経がこのまま駄目になってしまうんじゃないかと思うときもあった。私には物事の順序がわからなくなってしまっていた。私はただどんどん下に向かって落下していた。夜遅く私はそこに横になって、頭の中で不気味な映画がぱたぱたと進行していくのをじっと眺めていた。私は国境警備隊に追跡されてい

lights and barking dogs—I'd be crashing through the woods, I'd be
down on my hands and knees—people shouting out my name—
❶the law closing in on all sides—my hometown draft board and the
FBI and the Royal Canadian Mounted Police. It all seemed crazy
and impossible. Twenty-one years old, an ordinary kid with all the
ordinary dreams and ambitions, and all I wanted was to live the life
I was born to—a mainstream life—I loved baseball and hamburgers
and cherry Cokes—and now I was off on the margins of exile, leaving my country forever, and it seemed so impossible, terrible and
sad.

🎧A22

   I'm not sure how I ❷made it through those six days. Most of it I
can't remember. On two or three afternoons, to pass some time, I
helped Elroy get the place ready for winter, sweeping down the cabins and ❸hauling in the boats, little chores that kept my body moving. The days were cool and bright. The nights were very dark. One
morning the old man showed me how to split and stack firewood,
and for several hours we just worked in silence out behind his
house. At one point, I remember, Elroy put down his ❹maul and
looked at me for a long time, his lips drawn as if framing a difficult
question, but then he shook his head and went back to work. The
man's self-control was amazing. He never pried. He never put me
in a position that required lies or denials. To an extent, I suppose,

---

❶the law closing in on all sides: 当局が四方からじわじわ迫ってきて★close in on . . .は「～に接
近する、を包囲する」。　❷made it through . . .: ★make it through . . .は「(つらい状況) をやり通
す、生き抜く」。　❸haul(ing) in the boats: ボートをしまいこむ★haul in . . .は「～を引き上げる」。
❹maul: 大槌

た。ヘリコプターとサーチライトと吠える犬。私は死にものぐるいで森を抜けた。私はよつんばいになって身をひそめた。人々は私の名を呼んでいた。当局はあらゆる方向から私を追い詰めていた。我が町の徴兵委員会やらFBIやら王立カナダ騎馬警官隊やらだ。何もかもが気違いじみていて、あり得ないことのように思えた。私は二十一歳の、ごく普通の青年で、ごく普通の夢とごく普通の野心を持っていた。そして私の望んでいることと言えば、生まれついたとおりの、ごくまっとうな人生を送ることだった。私は野球とハンバーガーとチェリー・コークが好きだった。そして今や私は永遠に祖国を捨てて逃亡するかどうかの瀬戸際に立たされていた。それは私にはとても信じられないことだったし、悲しくおぞましいことだった。

　どのようにしてその六日間をもちこたえたのか、私にはわからない。私にはほとんど何も思い出せないのだ。どうせやることもなかったし、二、三日私はエルロイがロッジの冬支度をするのを午後に何度か手伝った。キャビンの大掃除をしたり、ボートをしまいこんだり、そういう体をこまめに動かせる雑用をやった。昼間は天気が良くて、ひやりとしていた。夜になるとあたりは真っ暗になった。ある朝、老人は私に薪を割って積みかさねるやり方を教えてくれた。そして我々は何時間か、家の裏手で何も言わずに黙々と作業を続けた。そのうちにエルロイは楔を打つ大木槌をふと下に置いて、私のことをじっと見た。彼の唇はあたかも何か難しい質問をするかのように開きかけた。でもそれから彼は首を振って作業に戻った。その男の自制心たるや実に驚異的だった。彼は決して無理にこじあけたりしなかった。彼は何かを誤魔化したり、否定したりしなくてはならぬような立場には決して私を追い込まなかった。私

his ❶reticence was typical of that part of Minnesota, where privacy still held value, and even if I'd been walking around ❷with some horrible deformity—four arms and three heads—I'm sure the old man would've talked about everything except those extra arms and heads. Simple politeness was part of it. But even more than that, I think, the man understood that words were insufficient. The problem had gone beyond discussion. During that long summer I'd been over and over the various arguments, ❸all the pros and cons, and it was no longer a question that could be decided by an act of pure reason. ❹Intellect had come up against emotion. My conscience told me to run, but some irrational and powerful force was resisting, like a weight pushing me toward the war. ❺What it came down to, stupidly, was a sense of shame. Hot, stupid shame. I did not want people to think badly of me. Not my parents, not my brother and sister, not even the folks down at the Gobbler Café. I was ashamed to be there at the Tip Top Lodge. I was ashamed of my conscience, ashamed to be doing the right thing.

🎧A23

Some of this Elroy must've understood. Not the details, of course, but the plain fact of crisis.

Although the old man never confronted me about it, there was

---

❶reticence: 無口、寡黙　❷with some horrible deformity: 何か恐ろしい奇形を抱えて　❸all the pros and cons: ありとあらゆる賛成意見 (pros) と反対意見 (cons)　❹Intellect had come up against emotion: ★直訳は「知性は感情の壁にぶつかっていた」。　❺What it came down to, stupidly, was . . .: 要するにそれは、馬鹿馬鹿しい話だが、〜ということに尽きた

は思うのだが、その無口さはある程度までは、ミネソタのこの地方の人々としては典型的なものであった。そこではまだプライヴァシーというものが重んじられていた。もし私がそこを何か恐ろしい尋常ならざる格好で —— たとえば四本の腕と三つの頭というような姿で —— 歩いていたとしても、その老人は口が裂けてもその余分な腕と頭のことは口にしないようにしただろうと確信している。単純な礼儀正しさということもある。でも、それだけではなかった。私は思うのだけれど、その男は理解していたのだ。ただ言葉を並べるだけでは不充分なのだということを。その問題は口先で是非を論ずるという領域をもう越えていた。その長い夏のあいだ、私は様々な議論を尽くしてきたのだ。ありとあらゆる賛成意見と反対意見。そしてそれは既に、道理理論を尽くして決着がつくような問題ではなくなっていた。知性は感情に阻まれていた。私の良心は逃げろと告げていた。しかしなにかしらの非理知的で強力な力がそれを押し止めていた。それは私を戦争に向けて押し出していこうとする重みだった。要するにそれは、馬鹿馬鹿しい話だが、体面のようなものだった。根が深くて、ホットで、切実で、愚かしい、体面という感情。私はみんなに悪く思われたくなかった。両親にも、兄にも妹にも、ゴブラー・カフェにたむろしている連中にさえもだ。私はこうしてティップトップ・ロッジにいることが恥ずかしかった。私は自分の良心が恥ずかしかった。正しいことをすることが恥ずかしかった。

　そのあたりの事情もエルロイはある程度理解していたに違いない。もちろん細かいことまではわからないにしても、私が危機に直面しているということだけはわかっていたはずだ。

　老人は私に対して正面きってその話は持ち出さなかったけれど、彼は

one occasion when he came close to forcing the whole thing out into the open. It was early evening, and we'd just finished supper, and over coffee and dessert I asked him about my bill, how much I owed so far. For a long while the old man squinted down at the tablecloth.

"Well, the basic rate," he said, "is fifty bucks a night. Not counting meals. This makes four nights, right?"

I nodded. I had three hundred and twelve dollars in my wallet.

Elroy kept his eyes on the tablecloth. "Now that's an on-season price. To be fair, I suppose we should knock it down a peg or two." He leaned back in his chair. "What's a reasonable number, you figure?"

"I don't know," I said. "Forty?"

"Forty's good. Forty a night. Then we ❶tack on food—say another hundred? Two hundred and sixty total?"

"I guess."

He raised his eyebrows. "Too much?"

"No, that's fair. It's fine. Tomorrow, though . . . I think I'd better take off tomorrow."

⌂A24

Elroy shrugged and began clearing the table. For a time ❷he fussed with the dishes, whistling to himself as if the subject had been settled. After a second he slapped his hands together.

"You know what we forgot?" he said. "We forgot wages. Those

---

❶tack on . . .: 〜を付加 [追加] する　❷he fussed with the dishes: ★直訳は「彼は食器を相手に忙しくしていた」。

一度すんでのところですべてを白日のもとに曝けだそうかというところ
までいった。それは夕方頃のことだった。我々は夕食を済ませ、コー
ヒーを飲みデザートを食べていた。私は彼に勘定のことを尋ねた。今ま
ででどれくらいになっているのかと。長いあいだ、老人は目をすぼめて
テーブル・クロスを見下ろしていた。

　「そうさな、基本料金は一晩五十ドルだ」と彼は言った。「食事は別に
してだよ。今日で四日めになる。そうだよな?」

　私は肯いた。私は財布の中に三一二ドル持っていた。

　エルロイはまだテーブル・クロスの上にじっと目を注いでいた。「でも
もそいつはシーズンの料金だ。だからまあある程度の割引はあってしか
るべきだと思うんだ」彼は椅子にもたれかかった。「いくらくらいだった
ら妥当だと思うかね?」

　「さあね」と私は言った。「四十ドルくらいかな」

　「四十でよかろう。一泊四十ドル。それにプラスして食事代だ。あと
百ドルってとこかな。あわせて二六〇ドルになるよな?」

　「そうなるね」

　彼は眉をひそめた。「高すぎるか?」

　「いや、高すぎはしないよ。それでかまわない。でも、そうだね……、
明日にはそろそろ出発したほうがよさそうだな」

　エルロイは肩をすくめて、テーブルの上をかたづけ始めた。しばらく
彼はばたばたと食器を洗っていた。これで話のかたはついたという風に
口笛を吹きながら。すぐそのあとで彼はぱちんと手を打った。

　「そうだ、ひとつ忘れていた」と彼は言った。「手間賃のことだよ。あ

odd jobs you done. What we have to do, we have to figure out what your time's worth. Your last job—how much did you ❶pull in an hour?"

"Not enough," I said.

"A bad one?"

"Yes. Pretty bad."

🎧**A25**

Slowly then, ❷without intending any long sermon, I told him about my days at the pig plant. It began as a straight recitation of the facts, but before I could stop myself I was talking about the blood clots and the water gun and how the smell had soaked into my skin and how I couldn't wash it away. I went on for a long time. I told him about wild hogs squealing in my dreams, the sounds of butchery, slaughterhouse sounds, and how I'd sometimes wake up with that greasy pig-stink in my throat.

🎧**A26**

When I was finished, Elroy nodded at me.

"Well, to be honest," he said, "when you first showed up here, I wondered about all that. The aroma, I mean. Smelled like you was awful damned fond of pork chops." The old man almost smiled. He made a snuffling sound, then sat down with a pencil and a piece of paper. "So what'd this ❸crud job pay? Ten bucks an hour? Fifteen?"

"Less."

---

❶pull in . . .: (金) を稼ぐ　★インフォーマルな表現。　❷without intending any long sermon: ★直訳は「長い説教をするつもりなどなしに」。　❸crud: くず

んたはいろいろと雑用を手伝ってくれた。だからここはやはり、あんた
が働いた時間ぶんを計算しなくちゃならん。あんたがこれまでやってた
仕事は時給いくらだったんだね？」

「合わない給料だったね」と私は言った。

「ひどい仕事だったのかい？」

「うん、かなりひどかった」

　それからゆっくりと、なるべく話がくどくならないように心がけなが
ら、私は豚肉工場での毎日の仕事について語った。始めのうちはただ単
に事実を並べているだけだった。しかし知らず知らずのうちに私は血の
塊のことやウォーター・ガンのことや、体に匂いが染み込んで、どう
やってもそれが落ちないというようなことについて話しこんでいた。私
は延々としゃべった。私は彼に、錯乱した豚たちが夢の中でキイキイと
声をあげることや、畜殺したり肉をさばいたりする音のことを話した。
そしてときどき喉の奥にべたべたとした豚の匂いを感じて目が覚めるこ
とがあるということも。

　私が話し終えたとき、エルロイは私に向かって肯いた。

　「うん、正直に言うとだな」と彼は言った。「あんたが最初にここに来
たときにさ、そんなところなんじゃないかとは思っていたんだ。その匂
いのことだよ。あんたはまるで、ポークチョップ中毒の人間みたいな匂
いがしたよ」。老人はもう少しで微笑みまで浮かべそうになった。彼は
鼻をふんと鳴らし、それから紙と鉛筆を手に腰を下ろした。「それでと、
ここの雑用を手伝ってくれた手間賃はいくらくらいになるだろうな。時
給十ドルかな？　それとも十五ドルかな？」

　「それじゃ多すぎるよ」

Elroy shook his head. "Let's make it fifteen. You put in twenty-five hours here, ❶easy. That's three hundred seventy-five bucks total wages. We subtract the two hundred sixty for food and lodging, I still owe you a hundred and fifteen."

He took four fifties out of his shirt pocket and laid them on the table.

"Call it even," he said.

"No."

"Pick it up. Get yourself a haircut."

🎧A27

The money lay on the table for the rest of the evening. It was still there when I went back to my cabin. In the morning, though, I found an envelope tacked to my door. Inside were the four fifties and a two-word note that said EMERGENCY FUND.

The man knew.

🎧A28

Looking back after twenty years, I sometimes wonder if the events of that summer didn't happen in some other dimension, a place where your life exists before you've lived it, and where it goes afterward. None of it ever seemed real. During my time at the Tip Top Lodge I had the feeling that I'd slipped out of my own skin, hovering a few feet away while some poor ❷yo-yo with my name

❶easy: 優に　❷yo-yo: ばか、あほんだら　★俗語。

エルロイは首を振った。「十五にしよう。あんたはここで二十五時間働いた。簡単だ。全部で三七五ドルになる。その中から食事代と宿泊費の二六〇ドルを差し引いても、私はまだあんたに一一五ドル借りということになる」

　彼は五十ドル札を四枚シャツのポケットからひっぱりだして、テーブルの上に置いた。

　「これで貸し借りなしだな」と彼は言った。

　「それはないよ」

　「取りなって。そして散髪でもしな」

　金はその夜ずっとテーブルの上に置きっぱなしになっていた。私が自分のキャビンに引き揚げたときにもまだそのままだった。朝になって、私は封筒が一枚ドアにとめてあるのをみつけた。封筒の中には四枚の五十ドル札と、短い手紙が入っていた。そこには「非常用資金」と書いてあった。

　その男にはちゃんとわかっていたのだ。

　二十年を経て振り返ってみて、私はときどきふとこんな風に思ってしまう。あの夏のあの出来事は実はどこか別の次元で起こっていたのではないだろうか、と。君が実際にそれを生きる以前に、君の人生が存在し、そして君が実際にそれを生きたあとで君の人生がそこに行くことになる場所で、ということだ。それは始めから終わりまで、私には現実にあったことには思えないのだ。ティップトップ・ロッジにいるあいだずっと、私は自分が自分の皮膚から抜け落ちてしまったような気分がしていた。自分から数フィート離れたところに浮かんでいるみたいなかん

and face tried to make his way toward a future he didn't understand and didn't want. Even now I can see myself as I was then. It's like watching an old home movie: I'm young and tan and fit. I've got hair—lots of it. I don't smoke or drink. I'm wearing faded blue jeans and a white polo shirt. I can see myself sitting on Elroy Berdahl's dock near dusk one evening, the sky a bright shimmering pink, and I'm finishing up a letter to my parents that tells what I'm about to do and why I'm doing it and how sorry I am that I'd never found the courage to talk to them about it. I ask them not to be angry. I try to explain some of my feelings, but there aren't enough words, and so I just say that it's a thing that has to be done. At the end of the letter I talk about the vacations we used to take up in this north country, at a place called Whitefish Lake, and how the scenery here reminds me of those good times. I tell them I'm fine. I tell them I'll write again from Winnipeg or Montreal or wherever I end up.

⌒A29

On my last full day, the sixth day, the old man took me out fishing on the Rainy River. The afternoon was sunny and cold. A stiff breeze came in from the north, and I remember how the little fourteen-foot boat made sharp rocking motions as we pushed off from

じだった。そしてそのあいだ、私の名前と顔を持ったどこかの哀れな間抜けが、まったく理解もできないし求めてもいない未来に向けてよたよたと歩を運んでいた。今でもまだ、私にはそこにいる自分の姿が見える。まるで昔のホーム・ムービーを見ているみたいに。私は若く、日焼けして、痩せている。私の髪はまだふさふさしている。煙草も吸わないし、酒も飲まない。色褪せたブルージーンをはき、白いポロ・シャツを着ている。私には、夕暮れ近くにエルロイ・バーダールの桟橋に坐っている自分の姿を見ることができる。空は明るくきらめくピンクだ。そして私は手紙を書きあげようとしている。その手紙の中で私は両親に向かって書いている。私がこれから何をやろうとしているか、何故そうしようとしているか、そしてそのことを率直に彼らと話し合うだけの勇気を自分が持たなかったことをどれだけ残念に思っているか、ということを。どうか怒らないでください、と私は書いた。私は自分の感情を少しでもわかってもらおうと努力した。でもそうするには私の言葉は不充分だった。それで私はただこう書いた。これはやらなくてはならないことだったのですと。手紙の最後に、私は以前私たちがよくこの北の国に休暇旅行に来たことについて書いた。それはホワイトフィッシュ湖というところだった。ここの光景は僕にかつての良き時代を思い出させる、と私は書いた。自分は元気であるし、ウィニペグなりモントリオールなり、何処かに身を落ち着けたらまた連絡する、と。

　最後の一日、六日めの日に、老人は釣りをしようといって私をレイニー河に連れ出した。よく晴れた肌寒い午後だった。北の方からはひやっとした微風が吹いてきた。桟橋を押して離れるときに十四フィート

the dock. The current was fast. All around us, I remember, there was a vastness to the world, an unpeopled rawness, just the trees and the sky and the water reaching out toward nowhere. The air had the brittle scent of October.

🎧**A30**

For ten or fifteen minutes Elroy held a course upstream, the river choppy and silver-gray, then he turned straight north and put the engine on full throttle. I felt the bow lift beneath me. I remember the wind in my ears, the sound of the old outboard ❶Evinrude. For a time I didn't pay attention to anything, just feeling the cold spray against my face, but then it occurred to me that at some point we must've passed into Canadian waters, across that dotted line between two different worlds, and I remember a sudden tightness in my chest as I looked up and watched the far shore come at me. This wasn't a daydream. It was ❷tangible and real. As we came in toward land, Elroy cut the engine, letting the boat ❸fishtail lightly about twenty yards off shore. The old man didn't look at me or speak. Bending down, he opened up his ❹tackle box and busied himself with a ❺bobber and a piece of wire leader, humming to himself, his eyes down.

🎧**A31**

It struck me then that he must've planned it. I'll never be certain, of course, but I think he meant to bring me up against the realities, to guide me across the river and to take me to the edge and to

❶Evinrude: ★船外エンジンの製造会社名。　❷tangible: 確固とした、触って確かめられる
❸fishtail: (車などが) しり振り走行する　❹tackle box: 釣り道具箱　❺bobber: 浮き

のその小さなボートが小刻みにかたかたと揺れていたことを私は覚えている。流れは速かった。前にも言ったように、我々のまわりには見渡すかぎりに世界が広がっていた。人の住まない未開の原野だった。森と空と水が、どこまでもどこまでも続いていた。空気には十月のぴりっとした匂いが感じられた。

十分か十五分、エルロイはボートを上流に向けて進めた。河面には小波が立ち、銀灰色に輝いていた。やがて彼は方向を転じてまっすぐに北に向かい、エンジンをフル・スロットルにした。私の体の下でへさきが持ち上がるのが感じられた。耳の中で風がうなっていた。そして旧型のエヴィンルード船外エンジンの音。しばらくの間、私は頭をからっぽにして、何も考えなかった。ただ顔にかかる冷たいしぶきを感じているだけだった。それからふとこう思った。我々はこうしているうちにカナダの水域に入っているはずなんだなと。二つの世界を隔てる水上に引かれた点線を越えて。顔を上げて、こちらに近づいてくる対岸をじっと見つめているうちに、私の胸は突然ぎゅっと締めつけられた。これは白日夢なんかじゃないんだ。これは紛れもない現実なんだ。岸に近づくと、エルロイはエンジンを切って、岸から二十ヤードほどのところでボートがゆらゆらと軽く揺れるにまかせた。老人は私の方も見なかったし、何も言わなかった。彼は身をかがめて釣りの道具箱の蓋を開け、下を向いて鼻唄を歌いながら、熱心に浮きと針金の先に糸を結びつけていた。

彼はこれを意図的に計画していたのに違いないという考えが私の頭に浮かんだ。もちろん確証はない。でも彼は私を現実というものに直面させようとしたのだと思う。河を越えて、私をぎりぎりの縁まで連れていって、私が私の人生を選択するのにつき添っていてやろうと思ったの

❶stand a kind of vigil as I chose a life for myself.

🎧A32

I remember staring at the old man, then at my hands, then at Canada. The shoreline was dense with brush and timber. I could see tiny red berries on the bushes. I could see a squirrel up in one of the birch trees, a big crow looking at me from a ❷boulder along the river. That close—twenty yards—and I could see the delicate latticework of the leaves, the texture of the soil, the browned needles beneath the pines, ❸the configurations of geology and human history. Twenty yards. I could've done it. I could've jumped and started swimming for my life. Inside me, in my chest, I felt a terrible squeezing pressure. Even now, as I write this, I can still feel that tightness. And I want you to feel it—the wind coming off the river, the waves, the silence, the wooded frontier. You're at the bow of a boat on the Rainy River. You're twenty-one years old, you're scared, and there's a hard squeezing pressure in your chest.

🎧A33

What would you do?

Would you jump? Would you feel pity for yourself? Would you think about your family and your childhood and your dreams and all you're leaving behind? Would it hurt? Would it feel like dying? Would you cry, as I did?

I tried to swallow it back. I tried to smile, except I was crying.

---

❶stand a kind of vigil: ★直訳は「一種の見張りに立つ」。　❷boulder: 丸い巨岩　❸the configurations of geology and human history: 地質学と人間の歴史が作りあげた模様　★ configurationは「配列、配置」。

だろう。

　私はじっと老人のことを見つめていた。それから自分の手を見つめた。それからカナダを見つめた。岸辺は藪や森林で鬱蒼としていた。藪の中には赤い苺の姿も見えた。樺の木の枝の上の方に一匹のリスがいるのも見えた。大きなカラスが岸辺の大きな丸石の上にとまって私を見ていた。そういうのがすぐ間近に見えた —— なにしろ二十ヤードだ。そして私は木々の葉の作りあげるデリケートな格子細工を見ることができた。大地の織物を、松の根本の茶色く変色した針葉を。地質学と人間の歴史の作りあげた模様を。二十ヤードだ。やろうと思えばやれるのだ。私は水に飛び込んで、人生を賭して岸まで泳いでいくことだってできるのだ。自分の中で、この胸の中で、何かがぎゅっと固く絞り上げられるのが感じられた。こうしてこの文章を書いている今だって、その締めつけられる感触を私は感じることができる。私は君に感じてほしい ——河を渡ってくる風を、その波を、その静寂を、鬱蒼と木々の繁った国境を。そして君はレイニー河に浮かんだボートのへさきに坐っている。君は二十一歳で、怯えている。胸の中は息が詰まるくらい強く締めつけられている。

　君ならどうするだろう？

　水に飛び込むか？　自己憐憫に耽るか？　君の家族や子供時代や夢や、あるいは君があとに残していくすべてに思いを馳せるか？　君の胸は痛むだろうか？　死んでしまうように感じられることだろうか？　君は泣くだろうか、そのとき私がそうしたように？

　私はそれを押しとどめようとした。私は微笑もうとした。でも結局私は声をあげて泣いてしまった。

Now, perhaps, you can understand why I've never told this story before. It's not just the embarrassment of tears. That's part of it, no doubt, but ❶what embarrasses me much more, and always will, is the paralysis that took my heart. A moral freeze: I couldn't decide, I couldn't act, ❷I couldn't comport myself with even a pretense of modest human dignity.

All I could do was cry. Quietly, not bawling, just the chest-chokes.

At the rear of the boat Elroy Berdahl pretended not to notice. He held a fishing rod in his hands, his head bowed to hide his eyes. He kept humming a soft, monotonous little tune. Everywhere, it seemed, in the trees and water and sky, a great worldwide sadness came pressing down on me, a crushing sorrow, sorrow like I had never known it before. And what was so sad, I realized, was that Canada had become a pitiful fantasy. Silly and hopeless. It was no longer a possibility. Right then, with the shore so close, I understood that I would not do what I should do. I would not swim away from my hometown and my country and my life. I would not be brave. The old image of myself as a hero, as a man of conscience and courage, all that was just ❸a threadbare pipe dream. Bobbing there on the Rainy River, looking back at the Minnesota shore, I

---

❶what embarrasses me much more, and always will, is . . .: ★私がそれよりずっと恥ずかしく思うのは、そしてこれからもずっと恥ずかしく思うにちがいないのは、〜ということだ　❷I couldn't comport myself with even a pretense of modest human dignity: ★直訳は「ささやかな人間の威厳の見せかけとともにふるまうことすらできなかった」。　❸a threadbare pipe dream: すり切れた夢物語

どうして私がこれまでこの話を誰にもしなかったか、その理由はおそらくわかっていただけるに違いない。涙を流したことに対する恥ずかしさからだけではない。もちろん言うまでもなくそれは理由のひとつではある。でもそれだけではない。私が何よりも恥ずかしく思うのは、そして、これからもずっと恥ずかしく思うにちがいないのは、自分の心が麻痺してしまっていたことに対してである。精神的冷凍状態。私には決断することができなかった。私には行動を取ることができなかった。たとえ見せかけだけでも人間としての威厳を保つことができなかった。

　私にできたのは泣くことだけだった。それも号泣ではない。胸を詰まらせるようなしゃくりあげだ。

　ボートのともの方ではエルロイがそれに気づかぬふりをしていた。彼は両手に釣り竿を持って、目があわぬように顔を下に向けていた。何かの歌を、ソフトな単調な声でハミングしていた。樹木や空や河のいたるところで、世界を圧するような大きな悲しみが私に向かってのしかかっているように思えた。それは圧倒的な悲嘆だった。私がかつて知ることのなかったような悲嘆だった。私がそれほど悲しかったのは、カナダが今や惨めな幻想と化してしまったからだった。それが私には理解できた。愚かしく、そして絶望的だった。それはもはや可能性としては存在しなかった。まさにそのとき、対岸を眼前にして、私は悟ったのだ。そうするべきだとわかっていても、私はそうはしないだろうということを。私は私の生まれた町から、祖国から、私の人生から泳ぎ去ることはしないだろう。私は勇気を奮い起こすことはないだろう。自分を英雄に、良心と勇気に溢れる人間にしつらえていたあの古い夢は、所詮空疎な幻想にすぎなかったのだ。レイニー河の水面で波に揺られ、ミネソタ

felt a sudden swell of helplessness come over me, a drowning sensation, as if I'd toppled overboard and was being swept away by the silver waves. Chunks of my own history flashed by. I saw a seven-year-old boy in a white cowboy hat and a Lone Ranger mask and a pair of holstered six-shooters; I saw a twelve-year-old Little League shortstop pivoting to turn a double play; I saw ❶a sixteen-year-old kid decked out for his first prom, looking ❷spiffy in a white tux and a black bow tie, his hair cut short and flat, his shoes freshly polished. My whole life seemed to spill out into the river, swirling away from me, everything I'd ever been or ever wanted to be. I couldn't get my breath; I couldn't stay afloat; I couldn't tell which way to swim. A hallucination, I suppose, but it was as real as anything I would ever feel. I saw my parents calling to me from the far shoreline. I saw my brother and sister, all the townsfolk, the mayor and the entire Chamber of Commerce and all my old teachers and girlfriends and high school buddies. Like some weird sporting event: everybody screaming from the sidelines, ❸rooting me on—a loud stadium roar. Hotdogs and popcorn—stadium smells; stadium heat. A squad of cheerleaders did cartwheels along the banks of the Rainy River; they had megaphones and pompoms and smooth brown thighs. The crowd swayed left and right. A marching band

---

❶a sixteen-year-old kid decked out for his first prom: 生まれて初めてのダンス・パーティーのために正装した十六歳の少年 ★be decked out for …は「〜のために着飾る」、promは「(高校生が学年末などに開く正式な) ダンス・パーティー」。 ❷spiffy: こぎれいな、かっこいい ★インフォーマルな語。 ❸root(ing) me on: 私を応援する

側の岸を振り返りながら、私は無力感がどっと押し寄せてくるのを感じた。溺れるような感覚だった。まるで船から水の中にころげ落ちて、銀色の波に押し流されていくような。私自身のこれまでの人生が小さないくつもの塊となって去来した。白いカウボーイ・ハットをかぶってローン・レインジャーのマスクをつけ、六連発の二梃拳銃を腰につけた七歳の少年の姿が見えた。ダブルプレーをするべく身をひねっている十二歳のリトルリーグのショートストップが見えた。最初のダンス・パーティーのために正装した十六歳の少年が見えた。白いタキシードに黒のボウ・タイに短くフラットにカットされた髪、磨きたての靴、すごく澄ましている。私の人生が根こそぎ河の中にこぼれ落ちて、渦を巻いて消えていくように思えた。私がかつてそうであり、そうであろうとしたもののすべてが。私は息をすることができなかった。私は浮かんでいることもできなかった。どちらに泳いでいけばいいのかもわからなかった。これは幻覚だったと私は思う。でもそれはどのような現実にも負けないくらいに現実的だった。遠い岸辺から両親が私を呼んでいた。私には兄や妹の顔が見えた。町のすべての人々の顔も見えた。市長も商工会議所のメンバー全員の顔も見えた。昔習った先生やガールフレンドや高校の同級生の顔も見えた。何かのろくでもないスポーツ・ゲームみたいにみんながサイドラインのところから叫び声をあげて、私を応援していた── どっと沸くスタジアムの歓声。ホットドッグとポップコーン。スタジアムの匂いと、スタジアムの熱気。レイニー河の岸辺ではチア・リーダーたちのチームがカートホイール（腕立て側転）をやっていた。彼女たちはメガフォンとポンポンを手に、日焼けした太腿を見せつけていた。観衆は右に左にと体を揺すっていた。マーチ・バンドが戦闘歌を演

played fight songs. All my aunts and uncles were there, and Abraham Lincoln, and **❶**Saint George, and a nine-year-old girl named Linda who had died of a brain tumor back in fifth grade, and several members of the United States Senate, and a blind poet scribbling notes, and LBJ, and Huck Finn, and **❷**Abbie Hoffman, and all the dead soldiers back from the grave, and the many thousands who were later to die—villagers with terrible burns, little kids without arms or legs—yes, and **❸**the Joint Chiefs of Staff were there, and a couple of popes, and a first lieutenant named Jimmy Cross, and the last surviving veteran of the American Civil War, and **❹**Jane Fonda dressed up as Barbarella, and **❺**an old man sprawled beside a pigpen, and my grandfather, and Gary Cooper, and a kind-faced woman carrying an umbrella and a copy of Plato's *Republic*, and a million ferocious citizens waving flags of all shapes and colors—people in hard hats, people in headbands—they were all **❻**whooping and chanting and urging me toward one shore or the other. I saw faces from my distant past and distant future. My wife was there. My unborn daughter waved at me, and my two sons hopped up and down, and a drill sergeant named Blyton **❼**sneered and shot up a finger and shook his head. There was a choir in bright purple robes. There was a **❽**cabbie from the Bronx. There was a slim young man I would one day kill with a **❾**hand grenade along a red clay trail outside the village of My Khe.

---

❶ Saint George: ★?-303 A.D.。 竜を倒したとされるイングランドの守護聖人。　❷ Abbie Hoffman: ★1936-1989。 ヴェトナム反戦活動を指揮し注目を集めたアメリカの政治活動家。 ❸ the Joint Chiefs of Staff: 統合参謀本部の人間たち　❹ Jane Fonda dressed up as Barbarella: ★『バーバレラ』は1967年にジェーン・フォンダ主演で映画化されたフランスの漫画家ジャン=クロード・フォレスト作のＳＦ漫画。ジェーン・フォンダはヴェトナム反戦運動をしていたことで有名。 ❺ an old man sprawled beside a pigpen: 豚小屋の横で大の字になっているひとりの老人

奏していた。私の叔父たちや伯母たちも全員そこにいた。エイブラハ
ム・リンカーンも聖ジョージも、小学校五年生のときに脳腫瘍で死んだ
リンダという名の九歳の少女も、何人かの合衆国上院議員たちも、メモ
をなぐり書きしている盲目の詩人も、そしてジョンソン大統領もハック・フィンもアビー・ホフマンも、墓所から戻ってきたすべての死んだ
兵士たちも、やがて死ぬことになる何千何万という数の人々も —— ひ
どい火傷を負った村人たち、腕や脚を失った子供たち —— そう、統合
参謀本部の人間たちもそこにいた、そして法王が二人ばかり、ジミー・
クロスという名の中尉、そしてこの小説の編集者、南北戦争従軍兵の最
後の生き残り、バーバレラの衣装に身を包んだジェーン・フォンダ、豚
小屋の横で大の字に寝ころんでいるひとりの老人、私の祖父、ゲイ
リー・クーパー、傘とプラトンの『国家篇』を持って歩いている親切そ
うな顔つきの女性。ありとあらゆる形と色の国旗を打ち振る何百万もの
凶暴な市民たち —— 作業用ヘルメットをかぶった人々、ヘアバンドを
した人々 —— 彼らは大声をあげ、スローガンを唱え、私をどちらかの
岸辺に追い立てようとしていた。私は私の遠い過去や遠い未来に属する
人々の顔を見た。私の妻がそこにいた。まだ生まれていない私の娘が手
を振っていた。二人の息子がぴょんぴょんと跳ねていた。ブライトンと
いう名の練兵係の軍曹があざ笑いながら指を一本立て、頭を振ってい
た。青い衣服を身にまとった合唱隊がいた。ブロンクス生まれのタク
シーの運転手がいた。ミケの村はずれの赤土の小道で、ある日私が手榴
弾を使って殺すことになる痩せた若者がいた。

---

❻whoop(ing) and chant(ing): 大声をあげ、スローガンを唱える　★whoopは「歓声をあげる」、
chantは「(スローガンなどを) 連呼する」。　❼sneered and shot up a finger: あざ笑いながら指を
一本立てた　★sneerは「あざ笑う」、shoot up a fingerは侮蔑的なジェスチャー。　❽cabbie: タク
シーの運転手　★インフォーマルな語。　❾a hand grenade: 手榴弾

The little aluminum boat rocked softly beneath me. There was the wind and the sky.

I ❶tried to will myself overboard.

I gripped the edge of the boat and leaned forward and thought, *Now*.

❷I did try. It just wasn't possible.

All those eyes on me—the town, the whole universe—and I couldn't risk the embarrassment. It was as if there were an audience to my life, that swirl of faces along the river, and in my head I could hear people screaming at me. Traitor! they yelled. ❸Turncoat! Pussy! I felt myself blush. ❹I couldn't tolerate it. I couldn't endure the mockery, or the disgrace, or the patriotic ridicule. Even in my imagination, the shore just twenty yards away, I couldn't make myself be brave. It had nothing to do with morality. Embarrassment, that's all it was.

And right then I ❺submitted.

I would go to the war—I would kill and maybe die—because I was embarrassed not to.

That was the sad thing. And so I sat in the bow of the boat and cried.

It was loud now. Loud, hard crying.

Elroy Berdahl remained quiet. He kept fishing. He worked his

---

❶tried to will myself overboard: 意志の力で自分を船外に動かそうとした　★willは「意志の力で〜する」の意の他動詞。　❷I did try.: やろうとはしたのだ　❸Turncoat!: 裏切り者　★=traitor
❹I couldn't tolerate it.: 私はそれに耐えられなかった　❺submitted: 屈伏してしまった

その小さなアルミニウム製のボートは私の下でゆるやかに揺れていた。風が吹き、空が広がっていた。

　私はなんとか自分自身の存在をボートから放り出そうとした。

　私はボートの縁を摑み、前に体を傾けてこう思った。さあ今だぞ、と。

　なんとかやってみようとした。でもそれはどうにも不可能なことだった。

　私の上に注がれたすべての目 ── その町、その宇宙 ── そして私はどうあがいても体面を捨て去ることができなかった。観客たちが私の人生を見守っているように私には思えた。河面じゅうにそういう人々の顔が渦をまいていた。人々の叫びが聞こえた。裏切り者！　と彼らは叫んでいた。腰抜け野郎、弱虫！　顔が赤くなるのが感じられた。私はあざけりや、不名誉や、愛国者どもに馬鹿にされることを我慢することができなかった。たとえ想像の世界だけでも、岸から二十ヤードしか離れていないその場所にあっても、私には勇気を奮い起こすことができなかった。それはモラリティーとは何の関係もない。体面、それだけのことだった。

　そしてそこで私は屈伏してしまった。

　俺は戦争に行くだろう ── 俺は人を殺し、あるいは殺されるかもしれない ── それというのも面目を失いたくないからだ。

　私は卑怯者だ。それは悲しいことだった。そして私はボートのへさきに坐って泣いていた。

　泣き声は大きくなっていた。私は声をあげて、激しく泣いていた。

　エルロイ・バーダールはじっと黙ったままだった。彼は相変わらず釣

line with the tips of his fingers, patiently, squinting out at his red and white bobber on the Rainy River. His eyes were flat and **❶**impassive. He didn't speak. He was simply there, like the river and the late-summer sun. And yet by his presence, **❷**his mute watchfulness, he made it real. He was the true audience. He was a witness, like God, or like the gods, who look on in absolute silence as we live our lives, as we make our choices or fail to make them.

"**❸**Ain't biting," he said.

Then after a time the old man pulled in his line and turned the boat back toward Minnesota.

🎧A38

I don't remember saying goodbye. That last night we had dinner together, and I went to bed early, and in the morning Elroy fixed breakfast for me. When I told him I'd be leaving, the old man nodded as if he already knew. He looked down at the table and smiled.

🎧A39

At some point later in the morning it's possible that we shook hands—I just don't remember—but I do know that by the time I'd finished packing the old man had disappeared. Around noon, when I took my suitcase out to the car, I noticed that his old black pickup truck was no longer parked in front of the house. I went inside and waited for a while, but **❹**I felt a bone certainty that he wouldn't

---

❶impassive: 無表情な、感情のない　**❷**his mute watchfulness: ★直訳は「彼の無言の目配り」。
❸Ain't biting: かからないな　**❹**I felt a bone certainty: はっきり確信した　★boneは「骨でわかる」という意味の形容詞として使われている。

りを続けていた。彼は指の先で釣糸をつまんで引きながら、忍耐強く、レイニー河に浮かんだ赤と白の浮きを横目で見やっていた。彼の目はフラットで表情がなかった。彼は口をきかなかった。彼はただそこにいるだけだった。河のように、晩夏の太陽のように。しかしその彼の存在は、その黙した視線は、それをとても現実的なものにしていた。彼こそが真の観客だった。目撃者だった。我々が自分の人生を生き、選択をしたり選択をできなかったりするのを絶対的な沈黙の中でじっと見守っている神のように、あるいは神々のように。

「食いつかんな」と彼は言った。

そしてほどなく老人は釣糸を引き上げ、ボートの船首をミネソタの方に向けた。

さよならを言ったのかどうか、私は覚えていない。その最後の夜、我々は一緒に夕食を食べた。そして私は早い時刻にベッドに入った。朝になってエルロイは私に朝食を作ってくれた。そろそろ引き揚げるよ、と私は彼に言った。それはわかっていたよというような顔をして彼は肯いた。彼はテーブルを見下ろして、そして微笑んだ。

昼近くになって我々は握手したかもしれない。私は本当に覚えていないのだ。でも私は覚えている。荷物をまとめ終えた頃にはもう彼の姿が消えてしまっていたことを。昼頃に、私はスーツケースを車まで運んだ。気がつくと建物の正面に停めてあった彼の黒のピックアップ・トラックが見えなくなっていた。私は家の中に入ってしばらく彼の帰りを待っていた。でも彼が戻ってはこないだろうということが、私には痛いほどにはっきりと確信できた。あるいはそのほうがいいのかもしれない

be back. In a way, I thought, it was appropriate. I washed up the breakfast dishes, left his two hundred dollars on the kitchen counter, got into the car, and drove south toward home.

🎧 **A40**

The day was cloudy. I passed through towns with familiar names, through the pine forests and down to the prairie, and then to Vietnam, where I was a soldier, and then home again. I survived, but it's not a happy ending. I was a coward. I went to the war.

な、と私は思った。私は朝食の皿を洗い、彼の二〇〇ドルを台所のカウンターの上に置いた。そして車に乗りこみ、家を目指して南に車を走らせた。

　その日は曇っていた。私は名前に聞き覚えのあるいくつかの町を通り抜け、松林を抜け、平原を横切った。それから私は兵士としてヴェトナムに行った。そしてまた故郷に戻ってきた。私は生き延びることができた。でもそれはハッピー・エンディングではなかった。私は卑怯者だった。私は戦争に行ったのだ。

A SMALL, GOOD THING

by

Raymond Carver

ささやかだけれど、役に立つこと

レイモンド・カーヴァー

　文学というものが凝った美文調で書かれるものではない、という思いはアメリカではもともと強い。そして19世紀後半に、マーク・トウェインが口語文体（日本風にいえば「言文一致」か）を導入してその思いを一気に加速させ、20世紀に入ってヘミングウェイが引き継ぎ、世界的な影響を与えた。アメリカ国内で見れば、ティム・オブライエンもレベッカ・ブラウンもポール・オースターも、それぞれ違いはあれ基本的に装飾を排したシンプルな文章は、ヘミングウェイの影響を抜きにしては考えられない。

　そのなかでも、ヘミングウェイ最大の後継者と思えるのがこのレイモンド・カーヴァーである。構文的にはきわめてシンプル、高校までの英語をいちおうちゃんとやった人なら、辞書を引く回数もそう多くなくて済むのではないか。

　とはいえ、ではそこで語られる世界は単純明快かというと、そうは行かない。カーヴァーの場合、特にいろんな物の表情が実に豊かである。医者の服装、廊下で見かける医療器具、パン屋がテーブルに置くバターやナイフ、天井で光る蛍光灯、それら一つひとつが、よそよそしかったり禍々しかったり、暖かだったり優しかったりする。といっても、「これは○○のシンボル」というふうにすっきり割り切れるわけでもない。その適度な能率の悪さが小説的に何とも雄弁である。（柴田元幸）

Saturday afternoon she drove to the bakery in the shopping center. After looking through a loose-leaf binder with photographs of cakes taped onto the pages, she ordered chocolate, the child's favorite. The cake she chose was decorated with a spaceship and ❶launching pad under a sprinkling of white stars, and a planet made of red frosting at the other end. His name, SCOTTY, would be in green letters beneath the planet. The baker, who was an older man with a thick neck, listened without saying anything when she told him the child would be eight years old next Monday. The baker wore a white apron that looked like a smock. Straps ❷cut under his arms, went around in back and then to the front again, where they were secured under his heavy waist. He wiped his hands on his apron as he listened to her. He kept his eyes down on the photographs and let her talk. He let her take her time. He'd just come to work and he'd be there all night, baking, and he was in no real hurry.

She gave the baker her name, Ann Weiss, and her telephone number. The cake would be ready on Monday morning, just out of the oven, in plenty of time for the child's party that afternoon. The baker was not ❸jolly. There were no ❹pleasantries between them, just the minimum exchange of words, the necessary information. He made her feel uncomfortable, and she didn't like that. While he

---

❶launching pad: (ロケット、ミサイルなどの) 発射台　★launch padとも。　❷cut under . . .: 〜の下を通った　★cutは「横断する、交差する」。　❸jolly: 陽気な、愛想のいい　❹pleasantries: 儀礼的な挨拶

土曜日の午後に彼女は車で、ショッピング・センターの中のパン屋に
でかけた。そしてルーズリーフ式のバインダーを繰ってページに貼りつ
けられた様々なケーキの写真を眺めたあとで、結局チョコレート・ケー
キに決めた。それが子供のお気に入りなのだ。彼女の選んだケーキには
宇宙船と発射台と、そしてきらめく星がデコレーションとしてついてい
た。反対側には赤い砂糖で作られた惑星がひとつ浮かんでいた。スコッ
ティーという名前が緑色の字で惑星の下に入れられることになった。パ
ン屋の主人は猪首の年配の男だった。来週の月曜日でスコッティーは八
つになるんです、と母親が言っても、ただ黙って聞いているだけだっ
た。主人はスモックのようなかたちの白いエプロンをつけていた。エプ
ロンの紐が両腕の脇から背中をぐるりと回って正面に出てきて、でっぷ
りとしたウエストの下で結ばれている。彼は女の話を聞きながらエプロ
ンで両手を拭いていた。そして見本帳の写真に目をやったまま、女に
ずっと喋らせておいた。パン屋は彼女にゆっくりと時間をかけてケーキ
を選ばせた。店を開けたばかりだったし、これから朝までそこでパンを
焼くのだ。何も急ぐことはない。

　彼女は自分はアン・ワイスという名前だと言った。電話番号も教え
た。ケーキは月曜日の朝にはちゃんと焼きあがります。午後のパー
ティーまでにはたっぷり時間の余裕がありますよ。彼は愛想のいい人間
ではなかった。冗談なんか言わない。手短に言葉を交わす。必要なこと
しか口にしない。バン屋は彼女を居心地悪い気分にさせたし、彼女はそ
れがどうも気に入らなかった。彼が鉛筆を手にカウンターにかがみこん

was bent over the counter with the pencil in his hand, she studied ❶his coarse features and wondered if he'd ever done anything else with his life besides be a baker. She was a mother and thirty-three years old, and it seemed to her that everyone, especially ❷someone the baker's age—a man old enough to be her father—must have children who'd gone through this special time of cakes and birthday parties. There must be that between them, she thought. But he was ❸abrupt with her—not rude, just abrupt. She gave up trying to make friends with him. She looked into the back of the bakery and could see a long, heavy wooden table with aluminum pie pans stacked at one end; and beside the table a metal container filled with empty racks. There was an enormous oven. A radio was playing country-western music.

The baker finished printing the information on the special order card and closed up the binder. He looked at her and said, "Monday morning." She thanked him and drove home.

⌁B03

On Monday morning, the birthday boy was walking to school with another boy. They were passing a bag of potato chips back and forth and the birthday boy was trying to find out what his friend intended to give him for his birthday that afternoon. Without looking, the birthday boy stepped off the curb at an intersection and was immediately knocked down by a car. He ❹fell on his side

---

❶his coarse features: その男の粗野な顔つき　❷someone the baker's age: このパン屋の主人のような歳の人　★the baker's ageの前のofはよく省略される。　❸abrupt: ぶっきらぼうな、つっけんどんな　❹fell on his side: 横向きに倒れた

でいるあいだ、彼女はその男の粗野な顔つきを眺めながら、この人はこれまでの人生でパンを焼く以外に何かやったことがあるのかしらと思った。彼女は三十三歳になる母親だった。そして世の中の人はみんな誰でも、とくにこのパン屋の主人のような歳の人なら（彼女の父親くらいの歳だ）、こういうバースデイ・ケーキや誕生パーティーといった特別な時代を通過してきた子供たちを持っているはずだと彼女は思っていた。私たちの間にはそういう共通項があるはずなのだと。なのにこの人はつっけんどんだ——無礼というのではないが、つっけんどんだ。彼女は親しく口を聞くのをあきらめた。パン屋の奥の部屋に、長いどっしりとした木のテーブルがあるのが見える。テーブルの端の方にはアルミニウム製のパイ焼き皿が積み重ねてあった。テーブルの隣には、空の枠をいくつも詰めた金属の容器がひとつ置いてあった。そして巨大なオーヴンがある。ラジオがカントリー・ミュージックを流している。

　パン屋は特別オーダーのカードに注文を書きつけ、バインダーを閉じた。そして彼女を見て「月曜の朝」と言った。お願いしますと言って彼女は家に帰った。

　月曜日の朝、誕生日を迎える少年は歩いて学校に行った。彼には連れがいた。二人の少年はポテトチップの袋を回していた。誕生日を迎える少年はもう一人の少年がプレゼントに何をくれるつもりなのか何とか口を割らせようとしていた。交差点のところで、誕生日を迎える少年はろくに注意もせずに歩道から下りた。そしてその瞬間に一台の車が彼をはね飛ばした。彼は横向きに倒れた。頭は溝の中につっこみ、両脚は路上

with his head in the gutter and his legs out in the road. His eyes were closed, but his legs moved back and forth as if he were trying to climb over something. His friend dropped the potato chips and started to cry. The car had gone a hundred feet or so and stopped in the middle of the road. The man in the driver's seat looked back over his shoulder. He waited until the boy got **❶**unsteadily to his feet. The boy **❷**wobbled a little. He looked **❸**dazed, but okay. The driver put the car into gear and drove away.

🎧**B04**

The birthday boy didn't cry, but he didn't have anything to say about anything either. He wouldn't answer when his friend asked him what it felt like to be hit by a car. He walked home, and his friend went on to school. But after the birthday boy was inside his house and was telling his mother about it—she sitting beside him on the sofa, holding his hands in her lap, saying, "Scotty, honey, are you sure you feel all right, baby?" thinking she would call the doctor anyway—he suddenly lay back on the sofa, closed his eyes, and **❹**went limp. When she couldn't wake him up, she hurried to the telephone and called her husband at work. Howard told her to remain calm, remain calm, and then he called an ambulance for the child and left for the hospital himself.

🎧**B05**

Of course, the birthday party was canceled. The child was in the hospital with a mild **❺**concussion and suffering from shock. There'd

---

❶unsteadily: よろよろと、ふらふらと　**❷**wobble(d): よろめく、ふらつく　**❸**dazed: ぼうっとした　**❹**went limp: 体から力が抜けた　**❺**concussion: 脳しんとう

にあった。目は閉じられていたが、脚は何かをよじのぼるような格好で前後に動いていた。連れの少年はポテトチップの袋を落として泣き出した。車は百フィートかそこら進んでから、道の真ん中で停まった。車を運転していた男は肩越しに後ろを振り返った。そして少年がよろよろと立ち上がるのを待っていた。少年は少しふらっとよろめいた。彼はぼんやりとした感じだったが、でも異常はないようだ。男はギヤを入れて走り去った。

　誕生日を迎える少年は泣かなかった。でもとくに言いたいようなこともなかった。もう一人の少年が、車にはねられるのってどんな感じだいと訊いても、返事もしなかった。彼は歩いて家に帰った。連れの少年はそのまま学校に行った。家に帰って誕生日を迎える少年は一部始終を母親に告げた。彼女は息子と並んでソファーに座り、その手を取って膝の上に載せた。「ねえ、スコッティー、大丈夫？　何ともない？」でも彼女はいずれにせよ医者を呼ぶつもりだった。そうするうちに突然、子供はソファーの上でごろりと仰向けになって、目を閉じ、ぐにゃっとしてしまった。どうしても子供が目を覚まさないことがわかると、彼女は夫の会社に急いで電話をかけた。ハワードは彼女にいいかい落ち着くんだ、落ち着くんだよ、と言った。そして救急車を呼び、自分も病院に急いだ。

　もちろん誕生パーティーは開かれなかった。少年は病院に運ばれた。軽い脳しんとうを起こし、事故のショックを受けていた。何度も嘔吐

been vomiting, and his lungs had taken in fluid which needed pumping out that afternoon. Now he simply seemed to be in a very deep sleep—but no ❶coma, Dr. Francis had emphasized, no coma, when he saw the alarm in the parents' eyes. At eleven o'clock that night, when the boy seemed to be resting comfortably enough after the many X-rays and the lab work, and it was just a matter of his waking up and ❷coming around, Howard left the hospital. He and Ann had been at the hospital with the child since that afternoon, and he was going home for a short while to bathe and change clothes. "I'll be back in an hour," he said. She nodded. "It's fine," she said. "I'll be right here." He kissed her on the forehead, and they touched hands. She sat in the chair beside the bed and looked at the child. She was waiting for him to wake up and be all right. Then she could begin to relax.

🎧**B06**

Howard drove home from the hospital. He took the wet, dark streets very fast, then ❸caught himself and slowed down. Until now, his life had gone smoothly and to his satisfaction—college, marriage, another year of college for the advanced degree in business, a junior partnership in an investment firm. Fatherhood. He was happy and, so far, lucky—he knew that. His parents were still living, his brothers and his sister ❹were established, his friends from college had gone out to take their places in the world. So far, he had kept away from any real harm, from those forces he knew ex-

---

❶coma: 昏睡 (状態)　❷coming around: ★come aroundで「意識を回復する」。　❸caught himself: はっと気づいて　❹were established: 地位を確立していた

し、両肺に水が溜まっていて、その日のうちに取り除く必要があった。子供はただぐっすりと眠りこんでいるように見えた。しかしそれは昏睡ではない。両親の目のなかにもしやという不安の色を読み取って、昏睡ではありませんよとフランシス医師は強調した。その夜の十一時、レントゲン写真をいっぱい撮られたり、いろんな検査を受けたあとで、少年はとても気持ちよさそうにすやすやと眠っていた。あとは少年が目覚めて、起き上がるのを待つだけ、というときになって、ハワードは家に帰った。彼とアンはその昼からずっと二人で少年に付き添っていた。だから彼はちょっと家に戻って風呂を浴び、服を着替えることにしたのだ。「一時間で戻るよ」と彼は言った。彼女は肯いた。「いいわよ」と彼女は言った。「私がここにいるから」彼は妻の額に口づけし、二人は手を触れ合った。彼女は枕もとの椅子に座り、子供の顔を見ていた。子供が元気に目を覚ますのを、彼女はじっと待ちつづけた。そうすればゆっくり休めるのだ。

　ハワードは車を運転して家に戻った。彼は雨に濡れた暗い通りをびゅんびゅんと飛ばした。それからはっと気づいてスピードを緩めた。それまでの彼の人生は順調そのものだった。それは満足のいくものだった。大学を出て、結婚して、もうひとつ上の経営学の学位を取るためにもう一年大学に行って、投資会社の下位共同経営者になっていた。そして子供もいる。彼は幸福であり、今までのところはラッキーだった。それは自分でもよくわかっている。両親は健在だったし、兄弟姉妹はきちんとした一家を構えていた。大学時代の友人たちは社会に出て、みんなそれぞれ立派にやっていた。これまで彼の身にはとりたてて悪いことは何も起こらなかった。そういう暗い力から、彼はずっと身を遠ざけていた。

isted and that ❶could cripple or bring down a man if the luck went bad, if things suddenly turned. He pulled into the ❷driveway and parked. His left leg began to tremble. He sat in the car for a minute and tried to deal with the present situation in a rational manner. Scotty had been hit by a car and was in the hospital, but he was going to be all right. Howard closed his eyes and ran his hand over his face. He got out of the car and went up to the front door. The dog was barking inside the house. The telephone rang and rang while he unlocked the door and fumbled for the light switch. He shouldn't have left the hospital, he shouldn't have. "Goddamn it!" he said. He picked up the receiver and said, "I just walked in the door!"

"There's a cake here that wasn't picked up," the voice on the other end of the line said.

"What are you saying?" Howard asked.

"A cake," the voice said. "A sixteen-dollar cake."

Howard held the receiver against his ear, trying to understand. "I don't know anything about a cake," he said. "Jesus, what are you talking about?"

"❸Don't hand me that," the voice said.

🎧B07

Howard hung up the telephone. He went into the kitchen and poured himself some whiskey. He called the hospital. But the child's condition remained the same; he was still sleeping and noth-

---

❶could cripple or bring down a man: 人の身を損ない (cripple)、引きずりおろしもする ❷driveway: 私有車道、アプローチ ❸Don't hand me that: そういう言い方はよせ

ツキが落ちて、いったん風向きが変われば、その暗い力は人の身を損ない、足をつかんで引きずりおろしもするのだということを彼は承知していた。彼はアプローチに入って車を停めた。左足ががたがたと震え始めた。そこに座ったまま、ここはひとつ冷静に対処しなくちゃなと彼は思った。スコッティーが車にはねられて入院している。でもまもなく回復するだろう。ハワードは目を閉じて手で顔を撫でた。それから車を下りて玄関まで歩いた。家の中で犬が吠えていた。彼が鍵でドアを開け、もそもそと壁のスイッチを探っているあいだずっと、電話のベルが鳴り続けていた。俺は家になんか帰ってくるべきじゃなかった。病院にいるべきだったんだ。「畜生！」と彼は言った。彼は受話器を取って「今帰ってきたばかりだよ！」と言った。

「ケーキを取りに来ていただかないと」と電話の相手は言った。

「何の話でしょう？」とハワードは訊いた。

「ケーキですよ」と相手は言った。「十六ドルのケーキです」

ハワードは話の筋を理解しようと、受話器をぎゅっと耳に押しつけた。「ケーキがいったいどうしたんだ」と彼は言った。「やれやれ、君は何の話をしているんだ？」

「そういう言い方はないぞ」と相手は言った。

ハワードはがちゃんと電話を切った。彼はキッチンに行って、ウィスキーを少しグラスに注いだ。そして病院に電話をかけてみたが、子供の容体は前と同じだった。子供は眠り続け、変わったことは何も起こって

ing had changed there. While water poured into the tub, Howard ❶lathered his face and shaved. He'd just stretched out in the tub and closed his eyes when the telephone rang again. He ❷hauled himself out, grabbed a towel, and hurried through the house, saying, "Stupid, stupid," for having left the hospital. But when he picked up the receiver and shouted, "Hello!" there was no sound at the other end of the line. Then the caller hung up.

🎧B08

He arrived back at the hospital a little after midnight. Ann still sat in the chair beside the bed. She looked up at Howard, and then she looked back at the child. The child's eyes stayed closed, the head was still wrapped in bandages. His breathing was quiet and regular. From an ❸apparatus over the bed hung a bottle of glucose with a tube running from the bottle to the boy's arm.

🎧B09

"How is he?" Howard said. "What's all this?" waving at the glucose and the tube.

"Dr. Francis's orders," she said. "He needs ❹nourishment. He needs to keep up his strength. Why doesn't he wake up, Howard? I don't understand, if he's all right."

Howard put his hand against the back of her head. He ran his fingers through her hair. "He's going to be all right. He'll wake up in a little while. Dr. Francis ❺knows what's what."

---

❶lathered his face: 顔にせっけんをつけた　❷hauled himself out: あわててバスタブから出た
❸apparatus:（科学・医学などで使われる）器具、装置　❹nourishment: 栄養　❺knows what's
what: 何がどうだかちゃんとわかっている

いなかった。風呂に湯をはっている間に、ハワードは髭を剃った。そしてバスタブの中で体を伸ばして目を閉じると、また電話のベルが鳴りはじめた。彼は立ち上がって風呂を出ると、タオルをつかみ、急いで部屋を抜けて電話のところにいった。「俺は馬鹿だった。まったく馬鹿だった」と彼は言いつづけていた。病院を離れるべきではなかったのだ。彼は受話器を取り、「もしもし！」と怒鳴った。電話の向こうには物音ひとつ聞こえなかった。それから相手は電話を切った。

　真夜中少し過ぎに彼は病院に戻った。アンは相変わらず枕もとの椅子に腰かけていた。彼女はハワードを見上げ、それからまた子供に視線を戻した。子供の目は閉じられたままだった。頭はまだ包帯に包まれていた。息づかいは穏やかで、規則的だった。ベッドの上の器具にはブドウ糖の瓶が吊るされ、そのチューブが少年の腕に繋がれていた。

　「具合はどうだい？」とハワードは訊いた。「これは何だい、いったい？」と彼はブドウ糖の瓶とチューブを指さした。

　「フランシス先生の指示なの」と彼女は言った。「栄養補給が必要なんだって。体力を維持する必要があるの。ねえハワード、この子どうして眠りっぱなしなの？　何ともないのなら、どうして目を覚まさないのよ？」

　ハワードは妻の後頭部に手をあて、指で髪を撫でた。「きっと良くなるさ。すぐに目を覚ます。フランシス先生にまかせておけば大丈夫だよ」

After a time, he said, "Maybe you should go home and get some rest. I'll stay here. ❶Just don't put up with this creep who keeps calling. Hang up right away."

"Who's calling?" she asked.

"I don't know who, just somebody with nothing better to do than call up people. You go on now."

She shook her head. "No," she said, "I'm fine."

"Really," he said. "Go home for a while, and then come back and ❷spell me in the morning. It'll be all right. What did Dr. Francis say? He said Scotty's going to be all right. We don't have to worry. He's just sleeping now, that's all."

A nurse pushed the door open. She nodded at them as she went to the bedside. She took the left arm out from under the covers and put her fingers on the wrist, found the pulse, then consulted her watch. In a little while, she put the arm back under the covers and moved to the foot of the bed, where she wrote something on a clipboard attached to the bed.

"How is he?" Ann said. Howard's hand was a weight on her shoulder. She was aware of the pressure from his fingers.

"He's stable," the nurse said. Then she said, "Doctor will be in again shortly. Doctor's back in the hospital. He's making rounds right now."

---

❶Just don't put up with this creep: 何はともあれ嫌な奴を我慢するな　★thisはこれからその人や物について説明するというニュアンス。　❷spell:（休憩などのために）～と交代する　★インフォーマルな表現。

少し間があって彼は言った。「君もちょっと家に帰ってひとやすみしたらどうだい？　そのあいだ僕が付いているよ。しつこく家に電話をかけてくる変態野郎がいるけど、相手にしないように。切っちまえばいいのさ」

　「誰が電話かけてくるの？」と彼女は訊いた。

　「誰だか知らないよ。いたずら電話をかけるくらいしか楽しみのない奴さ。さあ、家に帰りなさい」

　彼女は首を振った。「帰らない」と彼女は言った。「私は大丈夫よ」

　「なあ、頼む。ちょっと家に帰って休んで、また戻ってきて、朝に僕と交代してくれ。それでいい。フランシス先生はなんて言った？　スコッティーは元気になるって言っただろう？　だから心配することなんかないんだよ。スコッティーはぐっすり眠ってるんだ。それだけのことだよ」

　看護婦がドアを押し開けた。そして二人に向かって会釈してから、枕もとに行った。彼女は布団の中から少年の左手を出して、腕首に指をあて、時計を見ながら脈を取った。そして少ししてから手をまた布団の中に戻し、ベッドの足下に行って、そこでベッドに備えつけてあるクリップボードに何か書きこんだ。

　「具合はどうですか？」とアンが訊いた。ハワードの手は彼女の肩の上で重く感じられた。彼の手の指に力が入るのがわかった。

　「安定してます」と看護婦は言った。それからこう言い添えた。「まもなく先生がお見えになります。先生は病院に戻ってられて、今巡回してらっしゃるんです」

"I was saying maybe she'd want to go home and get a little rest," Howard said. "After the doctor comes," he said.

"She could do that," the nurse said. "I think you should both feel free to do that, if you wish." The nurse was a big Scandinavian woman with blond hair. There was ❶the trace of an accent in her speech.

"We'll see what the doctor says," Ann said. "I want to talk to the doctor. I don't think he should keep sleeping like this. I don't think that's a good sign." She brought her hand up to her eyes and let her head come forward a little. Howard's grip tightened on her shoulder, and then his hand moved up to her neck, where his fingers began to ❷knead the muscles there.

"Dr. Francis will be here in a few minutes," the nurse said. Then she left the room.

🎧B12

Howard gazed at his son for a time, the small chest quietly rising and falling under the covers. For the first time since the terrible minutes after Ann's telephone call to him at his office, ❸he felt a genuine fear starting in his limbs. He began shaking his head. Scotty was fine, but instead of sleeping at home in his own bed, he was in a hospital bed with bandages around his head and a tube in his arm. But this help was what he needed right now.

🎧B13

Dr. Francis came in and shook hands with Howard, though

❶the trace of an accent: わずかな訛　❷knead the muscles: 筋肉をこねるように揉む　❸he felt a genuine fear starting in his limbs: 彼は正真正銘の恐怖が四肢で生じるのを感じた

「今話をしてたんですが、妻はできたら帰宅して休みをとりたいんです」とハワードは言った。「先生が見えたあとででも」

　「どうぞそうなすって下さい」と看護婦は言った。「お二人ともお帰りになっても、べつにかまわないんですよ。もしお望みなら」看護婦は大柄な金髪のスカンジナビア系の女だった。彼女の喋り方には少し訛があった。

　「先生のおっしゃることを聞きたいわ」とアンは言った。「先生とお話ししたいの。この子がこんな風に眠り続けるなんて何だか変よ。良い徴候じゃないと思う」彼女は片手を上げて目にあて、少しうつむいた。肩に置かれたハワードの手に力が入った。それからその手は首の方に上がってきた。指が首の筋肉をこねるように揉み始めた。

　「フランシス先生はもうお見えになります」と看護婦は言った。そして部屋を出ていった。

　ハワードはしばらく息子の顔をじっと食い入るように見ていた。掛け布団の下で、その小さな胸が静かに上下していた。会社にアンから電話がかかってきたあの恐ろしい一瞬以来久し振りに、まぎれもない正真正銘の恐怖が彼の四肢を脅かした。彼は頭を何度も振った。スコッティーは大丈夫だ。でも彼が眠っているのは家のベッドではなく、病院のベッドだ。頭には包帯が巻かれ、腕にはチューブがささっている。でもそういう助けが今の彼には必要なのだ。

　フランシス医師が部屋に入ってきた。さっき会ってからまだ数時間し

they'd just seen each other a few hours before. Ann got up from the chair. "Doctor?"

"Ann," he said and nodded. "Let's just first see how he's doing," the doctor said. He moved to the side of the bed and took the boy's pulse. He peeled back one eyelid and then the other. Howard and Ann stood beside the doctor and watched. Then the doctor turned back the covers and listened to the boy's heart and lungs with his ❶stethoscope. He pressed his fingers here and there on the ❷abdomen. When he was finished, he went to the end of the bed and studied the chart. He noted the time, scribbled something on the chart, and then looked at Howard and Ann.

"Doctor, how is he?" Howard said. "What's the matter with him exactly?"

"Why doesn't he wake up?" Ann said.

🎧B14

The doctor was a handsome, big-shouldered man with a tanned face. He wore a three-piece blue suit, a striped tie, and ivory cuff links. His gray hair was combed along the sides of his head, and he looked as if he had just come from a concert. "He's all right," the doctor said. "Nothing to shout about, he could be better, I think. But he's all right. Still, I wish he'd wake up. He should wake up pretty soon." The doctor looked at the boy again. "We'll know some more in a couple of hours, after the results of a few more tests are in. But he's all right, believe me, except for ❸the hairline fracture of

---

❶stethoscope: 聴診器　❷abdomen: 腹、腹部　❸the hairline fracture: かすかな骨折、細いひび

か経っていなかったが、彼はハワードと握手をした。アンは椅子から立ち上がった。「先生？」

　「やあ、アン」と彼は言って肯いた。「まず坊やの様子を見てみましょう」と医者は言った。彼はベッドの脇に行って、少年の脈を取った。片方の瞼を開け、もう片方もおなじように開けた。ハワードとアンは医者の隣に立ってそれを見ていた。それから医者は布団をめくり、聴診器を使って心臓と肺の音を聴いた。腹のあちこちに指をあてた。それが終わると、彼はベッドの足下に行って、チャートを調べた。彼は時刻に目をやり、何やらチャートに記入していた。それからハワードとアンの方を向いた。

　「いかがですか、先生？」ハワードが尋ねた。「いったい息子はどうなっちゃってるんでしょう？」

　「どうして目を覚まさないんです？」とアンが言った。

　医者はハンサムで、肩が広く、顔は日焼けしていた。三つ揃いのブルーのスーツを着て、ストライプのネクタイをしめていた。そして象牙のカフスボタン。グレーの髪はぴたりと頭の両側に撫でつけられている。彼はまるで今しがたコンサートから帰ってきたばかりといった風情だった。「大丈夫ですよ」と医者は言った。「そんなに御心配なさるようなことはありません。もちろんまだ元気に回復したとは言えませんが、大丈夫です。目さえ覚めてくれればいいんです。時間の問題ですよ」医者はまた少年の方を見た。「二時間ほどしたら、もっと詳しいことがわかります。あといくつか検査をやって、その結果が出てきますから。でも御心配には及びません。信じて下さい。頭蓋骨にかすかなひびが入って

the skull. He does have that."

"Oh, no," Ann said.

"And a bit of a concussion, as I said before. Of course, you know he's in shock," the doctor said. "Sometimes you see this in shock cases. This sleeping."

"But he's out of any real danger?" Howard said. "You said before he's not in a coma. You wouldn't call this a coma, then—would you, doctor?" Howard waited. He looked at the doctor.

"No, I don't want to call it a coma," the doctor said and glanced over at the boy once more. "He's just in a very deep sleep. It's ❶a restorative measure the body is taking on its own. He's out of any real danger, I'd say that for certain, yes. But we'll know more when he wakes up and ❷the other tests are in," the doctor said.

"It's a coma," Ann said. "❸Of sorts."

🎧B15

"It's not a coma yet, not exactly," the doctor said. "I wouldn't want to call it coma. Not yet, anyway. He's suffered shock. In shock cases, this kind of reaction is common enough; it's a temporary reaction to bodily trauma. Coma. Well, coma is a deep, prolonged unconsciousness, something that could go on for days, or weeks even. Scotty's not in that area, not as far as we can tell. I'm certain his condition will show improvement by morning. I'm betting that it will. We'll know more when he wakes up, which shouldn't be

---

❶a restorative measure: 直訳は「元気を回復させる手段」。 ❷the other tests are in: 別の検査の結果が出る ❸of sorts: それほど大したものではないが

いる以外に悪いところはないんです。たしかにひびは入っていますが」

「そんな」とアンは言った。

「そして、以前にも申し上げたように、軽い脳しんとうを起こしています。言うまでもなく、彼はショックを受けています」と医者は言った。「ショックを受けたこういう例はたまにあるんです。眠りこんでしまうことが」

「でも大きな危険はないとおっしゃるんですね？」とハワードが言った。「これは昏睡じゃないってさっきおっしゃいましたよね？　たしかに昏睡ではないんですね、先生？」ハワードは答えを待った。彼はじっと医者を見ていた。

「そう、昏睡というのではありません」と医者は言って、またちらっと少年を見やった。「彼はとても深く熟睡しているのです。体は自らを回復しようとしていて、眠りはその手段なのです。大きな危険はありません。それは私がはっきり保証します。でも彼が目覚めて、検査の結果が出たら、よりはっきりしたことがわかります」と医者は言った。

「これはなんと言おうと昏睡です」とアンは言った。

「これはまだ正確には昏睡ではありません」と医者は言った。「これを昏睡と呼ぶつもりはありません。少なくとも今のところはね。彼はショックを受けているのです。ショックを受けた場合は、こういう反応が出るのはよくあることなんです。肉体的外傷に対する一時的な反応です。昏睡 ―― 昏睡というのは長期にわたる深い無意識状態です。それは何日も、ときには何週間も続くことがあります。私たちの見るかぎり、スコッティーはまだその領域には入り込んでおりません。朝になれば、回復の徴候が出てくるはずです。大丈夫、私が保証します。目が覚

long now. Of course, you may do as you like, stay here or go home for a time. But ❶by all means feel free to leave the hospital for a while if you want. This is not easy, I know." The doctor gazed at the boy again, watching him, and then he turned to Ann and said, "You try not to worry, little mother. Believe me, we're doing all that can be done. It's just a question of a little more time now." He nodded at her, shook hands with Howard again, and then he left the room.

🎧B16

Ann put her hand over the child's forehead. "At least he doesn't have a fever," she said. Then she said, "My God, he feels so cold, though. Howard? Is he supposed to feel like this? Feel his head."

Howard touched the child's temples. His own breathing had slowed. "I think he's supposed to feel this way right now," he said. "He's in shock, remember? That's what the doctor said. The doctor was just in here. He would have said something if Scotty wasn't okay."

🎧B17

Ann stood there a while longer, working her lip with her teeth. Then she moved over to her chair and sat down.

Howard sat in the chair next to her chair. They looked at each other. He wanted to say something else and ❷reassure her, but he was afraid, too. He took her hand and put it in his lap, and this

❶by all means:（許可・承諾などを表わして）どうぞ、ぜひ　❷reassure:（人）の不安をなくす

めたらもっと詳しいことがわかりますし、ほどなく目は覚めるはずで
す。いうまでもないことですが、御自由に行動なさって下さい。ここで
付き添ってらしても結構ですし、お宅にお帰りになって休まれても結構
です。でももしちょっとのあいだ病院を離れて息抜きなさりたければ、
遠慮したりはなさらないように。こうして付き添っているのが大変なこ
とはよくわかっています」医者は少年を検分するようにもう一度じっと
見つめ、それからアンの方を向いた。「物事を悪い方に悪い方に考えて
はいけません、お母さん。私たちを信じて下さい。できるだけの手は尽
くしているのです。もう少しの辛抱と思って下さい」彼はアンに向かっ
て肯き、ハワードとまた握手して部屋を出ていった。

　アンは子供の額に手をあてた。「少なくとも熱はないようね」と彼女
は言った。それからこういった。「どうしましょう、この子すごく冷た
い。ねえ、ハワード、こういうのってちょっと変じゃない？　ちょっと
触ってみて」

　ハワードは子供のこめかみに手を触れた。ハワードの呼吸はもう落ち
着いていた。「この状況ではとくにこれでおかしくないと僕は思うけど
ね」と彼は言った。「この子はショックを受けているんだよ。先生がそ
う言っただろう？　それに今検診したばかりじゃないか。スコッ
ティーの様子がおかしいようなら何か言ってるさ」

　アンは唇を噛みながら、しばらくそこに立っていた。それから彼女は
自分の椅子に戻って腰を下ろした。

　ハワードはその隣の椅子に座った。二人は顔を見合わせた。彼はもっ
と何か言って彼女を安心させたかった。でも彼だってやはり怖かったの
だ。彼は妻の手を取って自分の膝の上に載せた。そしてそれは彼の気持

made him feel better, her hand being there. He picked up her hand and squeezed it. Then he just held her hand. They sat like that for a while, watching the boy and not talking. From time to time, he squeezed her hand. Finally, she took her hand away.

"I've been praying," she said.

He nodded.

🎧B18

She said, "I almost thought I'd forgotten how, but it came back to me. All I had to do was close my eyes and say, 'Please God, help us—help Scotty,' and then the rest was easy. The words were right there. Maybe if you prayed, too," she said to him.

"I've already prayed," he said. "I prayed this afternoon—yesterday afternoon, I mean—after you called, while I was driving to the hospital. I've been praying," he said.

"That's good," she said. For the first time, she felt they were together in it, this trouble. She realized with a start that, until now, it had only been happening to her and to Scotty. She hadn't let Howard into it, though he was there and needed all along. She felt glad to be his wife.

🎧B19

The same nurse came in and took the boy's pulse again and checked the flow from the bottle hanging above the bed.

In an hour, another doctor came in. He said his name was Parsons, from ❶Radiology. He had a bushy moustache. He was wear-

❶Radiology: レントゲン科、放射線医学

ちを安らかにしてくれた。膝の上の妻の手。彼は彼女の手を取って、
ぎゅっと握りしめた。それから力を抜いて、普通に握った。二人はしばら
くそのまま座っていた。じっと子供を見つめ、ひとことも口をきかずに。
時々彼は妻の手をぎゅっと強く握りしめた。やがて彼女は手を引いた。
　「私、ずっとお祈りしてたの」と彼女は言った。
　彼は肯いた。
　彼女は言った。「お祈りのやりかたなんてもうほとんど忘れちゃった
と思ってたんだけど、やってるうちに思い出してきたわ。目を閉じてこ
う言えばそれでいいのよ。『神様、私たちをお助け下さい。スコッ
ティーをお助け下さい』って。あとは簡単だった。言葉がするする出て
くるの。あなたもお祈りしたら？」と彼女は言った。
　「僕ももうお祈りした」と彼は言った。「今日の午後も祈った。いや昨
日だな。つまり、君が電話をかけてきて、車で病院に来るまでの間に
さ。僕はずっと祈っていたよ」と彼は言った。
　「よかった」と彼女は言った。初めて彼女は認識したのだ。私たちは
二人一緒にこれに、このトラブルに巻き込まれているのだと。彼女はそ
もそもの初めから今の今までずっと、これは自分とスコッティーだけの
身にふりかかった問題なんだという風に思い込んでいた。彼女はそれに
気づいてはっとした。彼女はハワードをその中には入れていなかったの
だ。彼もずっとそこにいて、その手を借りていたにもかかわらず。この
人が夫で良かったとアンは思った。
　前と同じ看護婦がやってきてまた少年の脈を取り、ベッドの上に吊る
された溶液の流れ具合を点検した。
　一時間ほどしてから、別の医者がやってきた。新しい医者の名前は

ing loafers, a western shirt, and a pair of jeans.

"We're going to take him downstairs for more pictures," he told them. "We need to do some more pictures, and we want to do a scan."

"What's that?" Ann said. "A scan?" She stood between this new doctor and the bed. "I thought you'd already taken all your X-rays."

"I'm afraid we need some more," he said. "❶Nothing to be alarmed about. We just need some more pictures, and we want to do a brain scan on him."

"My God," Ann said.

"It's perfectly normal procedure in cases like this," this new doctor said. "We just need to find out for sure why he isn't back awake yet. It's normal medical procedure, and nothing to be alarmed about. We'll be taking him down in a few minutes," this doctor said.

🎧 B20

In a little while, two ❷orderlies came into the room with a ❸gurney. They were black-haired, dark-complexioned men in white uniforms, and they said a few words to each other ❹in a foreign tongue as they unhooked the boy from the tube and moved him from his bed to the gurney. Then they wheeled him from the room. Howard and Ann got on the same elevator. Ann gazed at the child. She closed her eyes as the elevator began its descent. The orderlies stood at either end of the gurney without saying anything, though once

---

❶Nothing to be alarmed about: 警戒（注意）するほどのことではない　❷orderlies:（病院の）看護人　❸gurney: ストレッチャー　❹in a foreign tongue: 外国語で　★tongue=language

パーソンズと言った。レントゲン科の医者だった。彼はもじゃもじゃとした口髭を生やしていた。ローファー・シューズにウエスタン・シャツ、ブルージーンズという格好だった。

「もう少し写真撮りたいんで、この子ちょっと下に連れていきますね」と彼は二人に言った。「もっと写真撮る必要があるんです。スキャンもやりたいし」

「なんですって？」とアンは言った。「スキャン？」彼女はその新しい医者とベッドの間に立ちはだかった。「レントゲン写真ならもう撮りたいだけ撮ったでしょう」

「申し訳ありませんが、もっと撮りたいんですよ」と彼は言った。「そんな大層なものじゃありません。ただもう少し写真が欲しいだけです。それから坊やの脳のスキャンをやりたいんです」

「神様」とアンは言った。

「こういう場合、いつもやることなんです」と新しい医者は言った。「どうして坊やがまだ目覚めないのか、我々もちゃんと調べておきたいんです。これ、ごく普通の手順ですから。御心配なさることじゃありません。すぐに下に運びますから」と医者は言った。

ほどなく二人の看護人が車輪付担架を押してやってきた。どちらも黒髪で肌が浅黒く、白い制服を着ていた。彼らは外国語でふたことみこと言葉を交わしてから、子供の手に付けられたチューブを外し、彼をベッドから担架に移した。そして車を押して部屋の外に出た。ハワードとアンは同じエレベーターに乗った。アンは子供をじっと見ていた。エレベーターが下降しはじめると、彼女は目を閉じた。看護人たちは何も言わずに担架の両端に立っていた。一度だけ片方が連れに向かって彼らの

one of the men made a comment to the other in their own language, and the other man nodded slowly in response.

Later that morning, just as the sun was beginning to lighten the windows in the waiting room outside the X-ray department, they brought the boy out and moved him back up to his room. Howard and Ann rode up on the elevator with him once more, and once more they took up their places beside the bed.

∩ B21

They waited all day, but still the boy did not wake up. Occasionally, one of them would leave the room to go downstairs to the cafeteria to drink coffee and then, as if suddenly remembering and feeling guilty, get up from the table and hurry back to the room. Dr. Francis came again that afternoon and examined the boy once more and then left after telling them he was coming along and could wake up at any minute now. Nurses, different nurses from the night before, came in from time to time. Then a young woman from the lab knocked and entered the room. She wore white slacks and a white blouse and carried a little tray of things which she put on the stand beside the bed. Without a word to them, she took blood from the boy's arm. Howard closed his eyes as the woman found the right place on the boy's arm and pushed the needle in.

∩ B22

"I don't understand this," Ann said to the woman.

国語で何かひとこと口にしただけだった。そして連れの男はそれに対してゆっくりと肯いた。

　朝になって、太陽がレントゲン科の外の待合室の窓を明るく照らし始める頃、少年は運び出されてきた。そしてもとのベッドに戻された。ハワードとアンはまた子供と同じエレベーターに乗って、またそのベッドのわきの椅子に戻った。

　一日じゅう二人は待ち続けた。でも子供は目を覚まさなかった。時折、どちらかが部屋を出て階下に行き、カフェテリアでコーヒーを飲んだ。そしてまるで自分がやましいことをしているような気分になって、テーブルを立って、急いで病室に戻ってきた。フランシス医師はその日の午後にまたやってきて、もう一度少年を検診し、容体は良くなっている、今にも目覚めるでしょうと言って帰っていった。看護婦が（昨夜とは違う看護婦だ）時折やって来た。それから検査室の若い女性がノックして、部屋に入ってきた。彼女は白いブラウスに白いスラックスという格好で、いろんなものを載せた小さな盆を持っていた。彼女はそれをベッドの脇にあるスタンドの上に置いた。そして何も言わずに、少年の腕から採血していった。その女が子供の腕の適当な部分を探して、そこに針をつきたてている間、ハワードはじっと目を閉じていた。

　「これはいったいどういうことなんですか？」とアンはその女に尋ねた。

"Doctor's orders," the young woman said. "I do what I'm told. They say draw that one, I draw. What's wrong with him, anyway?" she said. "He's a sweetie."

"He was hit by a car," Howard said. "A hit-and-run."

The young woman shook her head and looked again at the boy. Then she took her tray and left the room.

"Why won't he wake up?" Ann said. "Howard? I want some answers from these people."

Howard didn't say anything. He sat down again in the chair and crossed one leg over the other. He rubbed his face. He looked at his son and then he settled back in the chair, closed his eyes, and went to sleep.

🎧**B23**

Ann walked to the window and looked out at the parking lot. It was night, and cars were driving into and out of the parking lot with their lights on. She stood at the window with her hands gripping the ❶sill, and knew in her heart that they were into something now, something hard. She was afraid, and her teeth began to chatter until she tightened her jaws. She saw a big car stop in front of the hospital and someone, a woman in a long coat, get into the car. She wished she were that woman and somebody, anybody, was driving her away from here to somewhere else, a place where she would find Scotty waiting for her when she stepped out of the car, ready to say *Mom* and let her gather him in her arms.

❶ sill: 窓枠

「医師の指示です」とその若い女は言った。「言われたことをやってるだけです、私は。血を採ってこいって言われたら、血を採ってくるんです。この坊や、いったい何処がいけないのかしら？」と彼女は言った。「こんなに可愛いのに」

「車にはねられたんです」とハワードは言った。「礫き逃げです」

若い女は頭を振り、また子供の顔を見た。それから盆を持って部屋を出ていった。

「どうして目を覚まさないの？」とアンは言った。「私、誰かからきちんとした答えをききたいの、ハワード」

ハワードは黙っていた。彼はまた椅子に腰を下ろし、脚を組んだ。そして両手でごしごしと顔をこすった。彼は子供の顔を見て、それからまた椅子に落ち着いた。目を閉じ、そして眠った。

アンは窓際に行って、外の駐車場を見ていた。もう夜だったので、出入りする車はライトをつけていた。彼女は窓の前に立って、両手で窓枠を摑んでいた。そして私たちはいま重大な局面に、厳しい局面に立ちいたっているのだと直観的に思った。彼女は怖かった。そして歯はがたがたと音を立てたので、彼女はしっかりと顎を閉じなくてはならなかった。大きな車が一台病院の正面に停まって、ロング・コートを着たどこかの女が乗り込むのが見えた。自分があの女になれたらと彼女は思った。そして誰かが（誰でもいい）車でここからべつのところに連れさってくれるのだ。何処か、スコッティーが車から下りてくる自分を待ちうけていてくれる場所へと。「母さん」とスコッティーは言って飛んできて、彼女は息子をぎゅっと抱き締める。

In a little while, Howard woke up. He looked at the boy again. Then he got up from the chair, stretched, and went over to stand beside her at the window. They both stared out at the parking lot. They didn't say anything. But they seemed to feel each other's insides now, as though the worry had made them transparent in a perfectly natural way.

🎧 B24

The door opened and Dr. Francis came in. He was wearing a different suit and tie this time. His gray hair was combed along the sides of his head, and he looked as if he had just shaved. He went straight to the bed and examined the boy. "He ought to have come around by now. There's just no good reason for this," he said. "But I can tell you we're all convinced he's out of any danger. We'll just feel better when he wakes up. There's no reason, absolutely none, why he shouldn't come around. Very soon. Oh, he'll have himself ❶a dilly of a headache when he does, you can ❷count on that. But all of his signs are fine. They're as normal as can be. "

"It is a coma, then?" Ann said.

The doctor rubbed his smooth cheek. "We'll call it that for the time being, until he wakes up. But you must be worn out. This is hard. I know this is hard. Feel free to ❸go out for a bite," he said. "It would do you good. I'll put a nurse in here while you're gone if you'll feel better about going. Go and have yourselves something to eat."

---

❶a dilly of a headache: ちょいとした頭痛　❷count on . . .: ～を覚悟する　★count on . . .は「（何かが起こること）を確信する」。　❸go out for a bite: 食事を取りに外出する

ほどなくハワードが目を覚ました。彼はまた子供の顔を見た。そして椅子から立ち上がり、伸びをして、窓際にやってきて彼女の隣に立った。二人は外の駐車場を眺めた。ひとことも口をきかなかった。でも二人は互いの身の内をしっかりと感じていた。あたかも心労が二人をごくごく自然に透明にしてしまったみたいに。

　ドアが開いてフランシス医師が入ってきた。彼は今回は違うスーツを着て、違うネクタイをしめていた。彼のグレーの髪は頭の両側にぴたりと撫でつけられていた。髭は剃ったばかりに見えた。彼はまっすぐベッドに行って、子供の具合を見た。「もう元気になってなきゃならないんだ。こんなことになるわけないんだがな」と彼は言った。「でも御心配なさらないように。それははっきりと申し上げることができます。この子は決して危険な状態じゃありませんから。目を覚ましさえしたら、もう大丈夫なんです。覚めないわけがないんですよ、まったくの話。もうちょっとの辛抱ですよ。そりゃあまあ、意識が戻ったらちょいとした頭痛は感じるでしょう。それは覚悟して下さい。でも悪い徴候は何ひとつないんです。これ以上ノーマルにはなれないってくらいノーマルなんです」

　「じゃあ、これは昏睡ですね？」とアンは言った。

　医者はつるりとした頬を撫でた。「とりあえずそう呼びましょう。彼が目を覚ますまでのあいだね。でも奥さんも体を壊してしまいますよ。これじゃ身が持ちません。付き添いってのは大変ですから。家に帰って、食事でもなさらないと。もし御心配なら、お帰りになっているあいだ、看護婦を付けておきますよ。帰って何か召し上がりなさい」

"I couldn't eat anything," Ann said.

"Do what you need to do, of course," the doctor said. "Anyway, I wanted to tell you that all the signs are good, the tests are **❶**negative, nothing showed up at all, and just as soon as he wakes up he'll be **❷**over the hill."

"Thank you, doctor," Howard said. He shook hands with the doctor again. The doctor patted Howard's shoulder and went out.

🎧 B25

"I suppose one of us should go home and check on things," Howard said. "Slug needs to be fed, for one thing."

"Call one of the neighbors," Ann said. "Call the Morgans. Anyone will feed a dog if you ask them to."

"All right," Howard said. After a while, he said, "Honey, why don't *you* do it? Why don't you go home and check on things, and then come back? It'll do you good. I'll be right here with him. Seriously," he said. "We need to keep up our strength on this. We'll want to be here for a while even after he wakes up."

"Why don't *you* go?" she said. "Feed Slug. Feed yourself."

"I already went," he said. "I was gone for exactly an hour and fifteen minutes. You go home for an hour and freshen up. Then come back."

🎧 B26

She tried to think about it, but she was too tired. She closed her

---

❶ negative: 陰性の　**❷** over the hill: (病気など) 峠を越えて、快方に向かって　★口語。

「何も食べられません」とアンは言った。

「もちろんそれはあなたの御自由ですが」と医者は言った。「いずれにせよ、私は悪い徴候はまったくないっていうことを申し上げたかったんです。検査の結果は正常でした。変わったことは何もありません。だから坊やは目を覚ましさえすれば、峠を越えたも同然なんです」

「有り難うございました」とハワードは言った。彼はまた医者と握手した。医者はハワードの肩をとんとんと叩いて帰っていった。

「僕らのどちらかが家に戻っていろんなことをチェックした方がいいと思うね」とハワードが言った。「たとえばスラッグにも御飯をやらなくちゃならんし」

「近所の誰かに電話してよ」とアンは言った。「モーガンさんに頼んでよ。あなたが頼めば犬の餌くらい誰だってやってくれるわよ」

「わかった」とハワードは言った。それからややあって彼はこう言った。「ねえハニー、君がやったらどうだろう。君が家に帰っていろんな用事を済ませて、それからここに戻ってくればいいじゃないか？ 君のためにもその方がいいよ。僕が子供を見ている。考えてごらん」と彼は言った。「僕らがここで消耗しちゃったらおしまいだよ。この子が目を覚ましてからも僕らはしばらくここに残っていた方がいいだろうし」

「あなたが帰ればいいでしょう」と彼女は言った。「あなたが自分でスラッグに御飯をやってくれば。そして自分も食事してくれば」

「僕はもう帰った」と彼は言った。「正確に言って一時間と十五分、僕は家に帰った。君も一時間家に帰って、さっぱりとしてきたまえ。それから戻ってくればいい」

彼女はそれについて考えようとした。でも考えるには彼女は疲れすぎ

eyes and tried to think about it again. After a time, she said, "May-be I *will* go home for a few minutes. Maybe if I'm not just sitting right here watching him every second, he'll wake up and be all right. You know? Maybe he'll wake up if I'm not here. I'll go home and take a bath and put on clean clothes. I'll feed Slug. Then I'll come back."

"I'll be right here," he said. "You go on home, honey. I'll keep an eye on things here." His eyes were bloodshot and small, as if he'd been drinking for a long time. His clothes were **❶**rumpled. His beard had come out again. She touched his face, and then she took her hand back. She understood he wanted to be by himself for a while, not have to talk or share his worry for a time. She picked her purse up from the nightstand, and he helped her into her coat.

"I won't be gone long," she said.

"Just sit and rest for a little while when you get home," he said. "Eat something. Take a bath. After you get out of the bath, just sit for a while and rest. **❷**It'll do you a world of good, you'll see. Then come back," he said. "Let's try not to worry. You heard what Dr. Francis said."

∩ B27

She stood in her coat for a minute trying to recall the doctor's exact words, looking for any nuances, any hint of something be-hind his words other than what he had said. She tried to remember

---

❶rumpled: しわくちゃな   **❷**It'll do you a world of good: ★直訳すると「それはずいぶん役立つだろう」。

ていた。彼女は目を閉じて、もう一度それについて考えを巡らしてみよ
うとした。しばらくしてから彼女はこう言った。「じゃあ少しだけ家に
帰るわ。もし私がこうしてここでじっとこの子を見ているのをやめた
ら、この子は目を覚ますかもしれないものね。わかる？　私がいないほ
うが、この子、目を覚ますかもしれないわよね？　だから家に帰ってお
風呂に入って、着替える。スラッグに御飯をやる。それからまた戻って
くるわ」

　「僕はここにいるよ」と彼は言った。「家に帰りなさい、ハニー。じっ
とここで注意して見ている」彼の目はまるでずっと酒を飲み続けていた
みたいに充血して小さくなっていた。服はしわだらけだった。髭もまた
目立つようになっていた。彼女はその顔に手をやり、それから引っ込め
た。夫がしばらく一人になりたがっていることが彼女にはわかった。彼
は少しのあいだ誰とも話したくないし、誰とも心労をわかちあいたくな
いのだ。彼女はナイト・スタンドの上のハンドバッグを手に取った。彼
は妻にコートを着せてやった。

　「そんなに長くは帰ってないから」と彼女は言った。

　「家に帰ったら座って、少し体を休めるんだよ」と彼は言った。「何か
食べて、風呂に入りなさい。風呂から上がったら、座ってまたしばらく
じっと休むんだ。それでずいぶん楽になるはずだから。それから戻って
おいで」と彼は言った。「あれこれ気に病むんじゃないよ。フランシス
先生の言ったこと聞いただろう？」

　彼女はコートを着たまましばらくそこに立って、医者が何と言ったか
一言ひとこと正確に思い出してみようとした。聞かされた言葉そのもの
より、その裏に細かいニュアンスなり、仄めかしらしきものが隠されて

if his expression had changed any when he bent over to examine the child. She remembered the way his features had composed themselves as he rolled back the child's eyelids and then listened to his breathing.

She went to the door, where she turned and looked back. She looked at the child, and then she looked at the father. Howard nodded. She stepped out of the room and pulled the door closed behind her.

🎧 B28

She went past the nurses' station and down to the end of the corridor, looking for the elevator. At the end of the corridor, she turned to her right and entered a little waiting room where a Negro family sat in ❶wicker chairs. There was a middle-aged man in a khaki shirt and pants, a baseball cap pushed back on his head. A large woman wearing a housedress and slippers was slumped in one of the chairs. A teenaged girl in jeans, hair done in dozens of little braids, lay stretched out in one of the chairs smoking a cigarette, her legs crossed at the ankles. The family swung their eyes to Ann as she entered the room. The little table was littered with hamburger wrappers and ❷Styrofoam cups.

"Franklin," the large woman said as she roused herself. "Is it about Franklin?" Her eyes widened. "Tell me now, lady," the woman said. "Is it about Franklin?" She was trying to rise from her chair, but the man had closed his hand over her arm.

---

❶wicker chairs: 藤椅子　❷Styrofoam: (商標) スタイロフォーム　★発泡スチロールの一種。

いないかと思い巡らした。医者が身をかがめて子供の検診をしているときに、表情が変化を見せはしなかったかと懸命に考えてみた。子供の瞼をめくったり、呼吸に耳を澄ませているときの医者の顔つきを彼女は思いだした。

　彼女はドアのところに行って、そこで振り返った。子供を見て、それからその父親を見た。ハワードは肯いた。彼女は部屋を出て、ドアを閉めた。

　彼女は看護婦の詰め所の前を通り過ぎ、廊下の端まで行ってエレベーターを探した。廊下の端で、彼女は右に曲がって、小さな待合室に入った。待合室の籐の椅子には黒人の一家が座っていた。カーキのシャツとズボンという格好で、野球帽を後ろにずらせてかぶった中年の男がいた。普段着にサンダルという格好の大柄の女が椅子の中にだらんと沈みこんでいた。ジーンズをはいて何ダースという数のおさげに髪を編んだ十代の娘が椅子の上に横になって体を伸ばして、煙草を吹かしていた。彼女はくるぶしのところで脚を交差させていた。アンが中に入っていくと、一家はみんなで彼女をじろりと見た。小さなテーブルの上には、ハンバーガーの包装紙や発泡スチロールのコップが所狭しと並んでいた。

　「フランクリンのことかい」と大柄な女はもっそりと身を起こしながら言った。「フランクリンのことで何かあったのかい？」彼女の目はしっかりと見開かれていた。「さあ、言っとくれよ、お姉さん。ねえ、フランクリンのことなのかい？」彼女は椅子から立ち上がろうとした。でも男が彼女の腕を手で摑んだ。

"Here, here," he said. "Evelyn."

"I'm sorry," Ann said. "I'm looking for the elevator. My son is in the hospital, and now I can't find the elevator."

"Elevator is down that way, turn left," the man said as he aimed a finger.

🎧**B29**

The girl drew on her cigarette and stared at Ann. Her eyes were narrowed to slits, and her broad lips parted slowly as she let the smoke escape. The Negro woman let her head fall on her shoulder and looked away from Ann, no longer interested.

"My son was hit by a car," Ann said to the man. She seemed to need to explain herself. "He has a concussion and a little skull fracture, but he's going to be all right. He's in shock now, but it might be some kind of coma, too. That's what really worries us, the coma part. I'm going out for a little while, but my husband is with him. Maybe he'll wake up while I'm gone."

🎧**B30**

"That's too bad," the man said and shifted in the chair. He shook his head. He looked down at the table, and then he looked back at Ann. She was still standing there. He said, "Our Franklin, he's on the operating table. Somebody cut him. Tried to kill him. There was a fight where he was at. At this party. They say he was just standing and watching. Not bothering nobody. But that don't mean nothing these days. Now he's on the operating table. We're

「落ち着くんだ、イヴリン」と彼は言った。

「ごめんなさい」とアンは言った。「私、エレベーターを探してるんです。息子が入院してるんですが、エレベーターが見つからなくて」

「エレベーターならあっちだよ。左に曲がるんだ」と男は言って指した。

娘は煙草の煙を吸い込み、アンのことをじろっと見た。彼女の目は糸のように細くなった。そしてその厚い唇をゆっくりとはがすようにして煙をふうっとゆっくり吐き出した。黒人の女はだらりと首を横に倒し、アンから目を背けた。もう何の関心もないという風に。

「子供が車にはねられたんです」とアンは男に言った。言いわけをしなくてはならないような気がしたのだ。「脳しんとうを起こしていて、頭蓋骨に小さなひびが入っているんです。でも快方に向かっています。今はショック状態なんです。でもそれは昏睡の一種かもしれないんです。それでとても心配なの。その昏睡のことが。私、ちょっと家に戻ります。その間主人が子供に付き添ってくれているんです。かえって私がいないほうが子供は目を覚ますかもしれませんしね」

「お気の毒に」と男は言って、椅子の中で姿勢を変えた。そして頭を振った。彼はテーブルの上に目をやり、それからまたアンを見た。彼女はまだじっとそこに立っていた。彼は言った。「わしらのフランクリンは今手術台の上におるんです。誰かがあいつを切ったんだ。殺そうとしたんですよ。喧嘩に巻き込まれましてな。パーティーだったんです。あいつはただ見物してただけだってことです。べつにちょっかい出したわけじゃない。でも当世、そんなこともう関係ないんですな。それで、あいつは今手術台の上におるんです。わしらただ希望を持って、お祈りす

just hoping and praying, that's all we can do now." He gazed at her steadily.

🎧 B31

Ann looked at the girl again, who was still watching her, and at the older woman, who kept her head down, but whose eyes were now closed. Ann saw the lips moving silently, making words. She had an urge to ask what those words were. She wanted to talk more with these people who were in the same kind of waiting she was in. She was afraid, and they were afraid. They had that in common. She would have liked to have said something else about the accident, told them more about Scotty, that it had happened on the day of his birthday, Monday, and that he was still unconscious. Yet she didn't know how to begin. She stood looking at them without saying anything more.

She went down the corridor the man had indicated and found the elevator. She waited a minute in front of the closed doors, still wondering if she was doing the right thing. Then she put out her finger and touched the button.

🎧 B32

She pulled into the driveway and cut the engine. She closed her eyes and leaned her head against the wheel for a minute. She listened to the ticking sounds the engine made as it began to cool. Then she got out of the car. She could hear the dog barking inside

るしかない。それ以外になんともしようがないのですわ」彼はじっと彼
女に視線を注いでいた。

　アンはまた娘に目をやった。娘はまだ彼女のことをじっと見ていた。
それからアンはがっくりと顔を伏せ続けている中年の女のほうを見た。
でも彼女は今は目を閉じていた。彼女の唇が音もなく動いて、何かの言
葉を形作るのが見えた。彼女が何と言ったのか、アンは聞きたくてたま
らなかった。彼女は自分と同じようにじっと待ちつづけているこの一家
ともっと言葉を交わしたかった。彼女は怯えていたし、同じようにこの
一家も怯えていた。彼らには共通点があった。彼女は事故についてもっ
と別のことを喋りたかった。スコッティーについてもっともっと話した
かった。それがこともあろうに彼の誕生日である月曜日に起こったのだ
ということも。そして彼はいまだに意識がない。でもどういう風に話し
はじめればいいのかがわからなかった。彼女はそれ以上何も言えないま
ま、ただじっと一家を眺め続けた。

　彼女は男が教えてくれたとおりに廊下を進んで、エレベーターを見つ
けた。彼女は閉じたドアの前にしばらく立ったまま、本当にこんなこと
をしてていいのかしら、とずっと考えつづけていた。それから彼女は指
でエレベーターのボタンを押した。

　彼女は家のアプローチに入ると、車のエンジンを切った。そして目を
閉じ、しばらくハンドルに頭をもたせかけていた。エンジンが冷えてい
くコチコチという音が聞こえた。それから彼女は車から下りた。家の中

the house. She went to the front door, which was unlocked. She went inside and turned on lights and put on a kettle of water for tea. She opened some dog food and fed Slug on the back porch. The dog ate ❶in hungry little smacks. It kept running into the kitchen to see that she was going to stay. As she sat down on the sofa with her tea, the telephone rang.

🎧B33

"Yes!" she said as she answered. "Hello!"

"Mrs Weiss," a man's voice said. It was five o'clock in the morning, and she thought she could hear machinery or equipment of some kind in the background.

"Yes, yes! What is it?" she said. "This is Mrs Weiss. This is she. What is it, please?" She listened to whatever it was in the background. "Is it Scotty, for Christ's sake?"

"Scotty," the man's voice said. "It's about Scotty, yes. It has to do with Scotty, that problem. Have you forgotten about Scotty?" the man said. Then he hung up.

🎧B34

She dialed the hospital's number and asked for the third floor. She demanded information about her son from the nurse who answered the telephone. Then she asked to speak to her husband. It was, she said, an emergency.

She waited, turning the telephone cord in her fingers. She closed her eyes and felt sick at her stomach. She would have to make her-

❶in hungry little smacks: いかにも腹を減らしたようにぺちゃぺちゃと小さな音を立てて

で犬が吠えていた。玄関のドアには鍵がかかっていなかった。彼女は家に入って電気をつけ、お茶を入れようと湯を沸かした。ドッグ・フードの缶を開け、裏のポーチでスラッグに与えた。犬はいかにも腹を減らしたようにぺちゃぺちゃという小さな音を立てて食べた。そして何度もキッチンの中に走りこんできて、彼女がまた出ていくんじゃないかと探っていた。お茶を手にソファーに腰を下ろしたときに電話のベルが鳴った。

「はい！」と彼女は急いで言った。「もしもし！」

「ミセス・ワイス」と男の声が言った。それは朝の五時だった。電話の背後で何か機械なり装置なりの音が聞こえたような気がした。

「はい、もしもし、何ですか？」と彼女は言った。「こちらはワイスです。ミセス・ワイスです。何の御用でしょうか？」後ろで聞こえるのは何の音だろうと彼女は耳を澄ませた。「スコッティーのことでしょうか？　どうなんですか？」

「スコッティー」と男の声が言った。「そうだよ、スコッティーのことだよ。そうだよ、スコッティーのことが問題なんだよ。あんた、スコッティーのことを忘れちゃったのかい？」と男は言った。そしてがちゃんと電話を切った。

彼女は病院に電話をかけ、三階を呼び出した。彼女は電話にでた看護婦に子供の状態を尋ねた。それから夫を呼んでほしいと言った。緊急のことなんです、と彼女は言った。

彼女は電話のコードを指にくるくると巻きつけながら夫が出るのを待った。目を閉じると胸がむかむかした。でも何か無理にでも食べなく

self eat. Slug came in from the back porch and lay down near her feet. He wagged his tail. She pulled at his ear while he licked her fingers. Howard was on the line.

🎧 B35

"Somebody just called here," she said. She twisted the telephone cord. "He said it was about Scotty," she cried.

"Scotty's fine," Howard told her. "I mean, he's still sleeping. There's been no change. The nurse has been in twice since you've been gone. A nurse or else a doctor. He's all right. "

"This man called. He said it was about Scotty," she told him.

"Honey, you rest for a little while, you need the rest. It must be that same caller I had. Just forget it. Come back down here after you've rested. Then we'll have breakfast or something."

🎧 B36

"Breakfast," she said. "I don't want any breakfast."

"You know what I mean," he said. "Juice, something. I don't know. I don't know anything, Ann. Jesus, I'm not hungry, either. Ann, it's hard to talk now. I'm standing here at the desk. Dr. Francis is coming again at eight o'clock this morning. He's going to have something to tell us then, something more definite. That's what one of the nurses said. She didn't know any more than that. Ann? Honey, maybe we'll know something more then. At eight o'clock. Come back here before eight. Meanwhile, I'm right here

ては。スラッグが裏のポーチからやってきて、足下に横になった。犬は
ぱたぱたと尻尾を振っていた。彼女が犬の耳を引っ張ると、犬はその指
をぺろぺろと嘗めた。ハワードが電話に出た。

「誰かが今電話をかけてきたの」と彼女は言った。彼女は電話のコー
ドをねじっていた。「スコッティーのことだってその人は言うのよ」と
彼女は叫んだ。

「スコッティーなら大丈夫だよ」とハワードは言った。「まだ眠り続け
てるってことだけどね。変化は何もない。君がいなくなってから看護婦が
二回やってきた。看護婦か、あるいは医者がね。スコッティーは問題ない」

「その男は電話をかけてきたのよ。そしてスコッティーのことだって
言ったの」と彼女は言った。

「ねえ、ハニー、君は休まなくちゃ。休むことが必要なんだ。そいつ
はたぶん僕が出たのと同じ電話の奴だろう。忘れちゃいな。休んだらこ
こに戻っておいで。そしたら二人で朝飯なり何飯なりを食べよう」

「朝御飯」と彼女は言った。「私、朝御飯なんて食べたくない」

「僕の言ってることわかるだろう？」と彼は言った。「ジュースとか、
そういうのでいいんだ。何でもいい。よくわからないよ、僕には。ね
え、アン、僕だって腹なんて減ってないんだ。ここでは話せないよ、ア
ン。僕はデスクの前に立ってるんだ。フランシス先生が八時にまたやっ
てくる。そこで何か我々に言うことがあるそうだ。もっとはっきりとし
たことが聞けるらしい。看護婦の一人がそう言っていた。彼女にもそれ
以上のことはわからない。ねえアン、そのときにもう少し詳しいことが
わかるだろう。八時だよ。八時前にこっちに戻っておいで。とにかく僕
はここにいるし、スコッティーは問題ない。ずっと同じ調子だよ」と彼

and Scotty's all right. He's still the same," he added.

"I was drinking a cup of tea," she said, "when the telephone rang. They said it was about Scotty. There was a noise in the background. Was there a noise in the background on that call you had, Howard?"

"I don't remember," he said. "Maybe the driver of the car, maybe he's a psychopath and found out about Scotty somehow. But I'm here with him. Just rest like you were going to do. Take a bath and come back by seven or so, and we'll talk to the doctor together when he gets here. It's going to be all right, honey. I'm here, and there are doctors and nurses around. They say his condition is stable. "

"I'm scared to death," she said.

🎧 **B37**

She ran water, undressed, and got into the tub. She washed and dried quickly, not taking the time to wash her hair. She put on clean underwear, wool slacks, and a sweater. She went into the living room, where the dog looked up at her and let its tail thump once against the floor. It was just starting to get light outside when she went out to the car.

She drove into the parking lot of the hospital and found a space close to the front door. She felt she was in some obscure way responsible for what had happened to the child. She let her thoughts move to the Negro family. She remembered the name Franklin and

は付け加えた。

　「お茶を飲んでいたら電話が鳴ったの」と彼女は言った。「そしてスコッティーのことだって言うの。後ろで何か音が聞こえるの。あなたの電話のときも後ろで音が聞こえたかしら?」

　「覚えてないな」と彼は言った。「その車を運転していた奴かもしれない。あるいは何処かの変質者がどこかでスコッティーのことを聞きつけたのかもしれない。でも僕はちゃんとスコッティーのそばにいるよ。だから予定通りにちゃんと休みなさい。風呂に入って、七時頃までにこちらに戻ってくればいいんだ。そして先生が来たら、二人で説明を聞こうじゃないか。何もかもうまくいくさ、ハニー。僕はちゃんとここにいるし、看護婦も先生も待機している。みんな容体は順調だって言ってる」

　「私、怖くて怖くて仕方ないの」と彼女は言った。

　彼女は風呂に湯を入れ、服を脱ぎ、バスタブに身を沈めた。体を洗い、手早くタオルで拭いた。時間がないので髪は洗わなかった。新しい下着を身につけ、ウールのスラックスをはき、セーターを着た。居間に行くと、犬が見上げて、尻尾を一度ぱたっと床に打ちつけた。外に出て車に向かう頃、空は白み始めていた。

　彼女は病院の駐車場に車を入れ、玄関の近くに空いた場所をみつけた。彼女は子供の身に起こったことに対して自分に漠然とした責任があるような感じがした。彼女はふと黒人の一家のことを思った。フランクリンという名前と、ハンバーガーの包装紙のちらばったテーブルのこと

the table that was covered with hamburger papers, and the teen-aged girl staring at her as she drew on her cigarette. "Don't have children," she told the girl's image as she entered the front door of the hospital. "For God's sake, don't."

🎧B38

She took the elevator up to the third floor with two nurses who were just going on duty. It was Wednesday morning, a few minutes before seven. ❶There was a page for a Dr. Madison as the elevator doors slid open on the third floor. She got off behind the nurses, who turned in the other direction and continued the conversation she had interrupted when she'd gotten into the elevator. She walked down the corridor to the little ❷alcove where the Negro family had been waiting. They were gone now, but the chairs were scattered in such a way that it looked as if people had just jumped up from them the minute before. The tabletop was cluttered with the same cups and papers, the ashtray was filled with cigarette butts.

🎧B39

She stopped at the nurses' station. A nurse was standing behind the counter, brushing her hair and yawning.

"There was a Negro boy in surgery last night," Ann said. "Franklin was his name. His family was in the waiting room. I'd like to inquire about his condition."

A nurse who was sitting at a desk behind the counter looked up

---

❶There was a page for a Dr. Madison: ドクター・マディソンなる人物の呼び出し放送があった
❷alcove: 小部屋、アルコーブ　★壁の一部を入り込ませた空間。

を思い出した。そして煙草の煙を吸い込みながらじっと自分を見ていた十代の娘のことを。「子供なんて持つもんじゃない」と彼女は病院の玄関に入りながら、頭の中の娘の像に向かって言った。「本当よ。持つもんじゃない」

　彼女は今から勤務に就こうとする二人の看護婦と一緒にエレベーターに乗って、三階に上がった。水曜日の朝、時刻はあと数分で七時になろうとしていた。三階でエレベーターのドアが開いたとき、ドクター・マディソンの呼び出し放送があった。看護婦たちのあとから彼女はエレベーターを下りた。看護婦たちは彼女と別の方向に歩いていきながら、彼女が乗り込んできたことによって中断されていた会話の続きを始めた。彼女は廊下を歩いて、黒人の一家が待機していた小部屋の前に行った。一家の姿はもうなかったが、まるでほんのちょっと前にみんなが飛び上がって何処かに駆けていってしまったという風に椅子が散乱していた。テーブルの上には前と同じコップと紙が散らばり、灰皿は吸殻でいっぱいになっていた。
　彼女は看護婦詰め所に寄った。受付カウンターの後ろに立った看護婦は髪をとかしながらあくびをしていた。
　「黒人の少年が昨夜手術を受けていたはずなんですが」とアンは言った。「名前はフランクリンです。御家族が待合室にいらっしゃってた方。手術はどうなりました？」
　カウンターの後ろのデスクに座っていた看護婦は目の前のチャートか

from a chart in front of her. The telephone buzzed and she picked up the receiver, but she kept her eyes on Ann.

"He passed away," said the nurse at the counter. The nurse held the hairbrush and kept looking at her. "Are you a friend of the family or what?"

"I met the family last night," Ann said. "My own son is in the hospital. I guess he's in shock. We don't know for sure what's wrong. I just wondered about Franklin, that's all. Thank you." She moved down the corridor. Elevator doors the same color as the walls slid open and a gaunt, bald man in white pants and white canvas shoes pulled a heavy cart off the elevator. She hadn't noticed these doors last night. The man wheeled the cart out into the corridor and stopped in front of the room nearest the elevator and consulted a clipboard. Then he reached down and slid a tray out of the cart. He rapped lightly on the door and entered the room. She could smell the unpleasant odors of warm food as she passed the cart. She hurried on without looking at any of the nurses and pushed open the door to the child's room.

⌒ B40

Howard was standing at the window with his hands behind his back. He turned around as she came in.

"How is he?" she said. She went over to the bed. She dropped her purse on the floor beside the nightstand. It seemed to her she had been gone a long time. She touched the child's face. "Howard?"

ら顔を上げた。電話のブザーが鳴って、彼女は受話器を取った。しかし彼女の目はじっとアンに注がれていた。

　「亡くなりました」とカウンターの看護婦が言った。彼女はヘアブラシを持ったままじっとアンを見ていた。「あの御家族のお知り合いか何かなんですか？」

　「昨夜、あの方たちに会ったんです」とアンは言った。「私の子供もここに入院しています。ショック状態にあるみたいなんです。何処がいけないのか、まだわからないんです。フランクリンのことが気がかりだったんです。それだけです。どうも有り難う」彼女は廊下をそのまま歩いていった。壁と同じ色をしたエレベーターのドアがさっと横に開いて、白いズボンに白いキャンバス・シューズという格好のやせて禿げた男が、重そうなカートをひっぱって下ろした。そんなドアがあることに、昨夜、彼女は気がつかなかった。男はカートを押して廊下に出し、エレベーターからいちばん近い部屋の前に止めて、クリップボードを点検した。それから彼は身をかがめてカートからトレイをひとつ取り出した。そしてこんこんと軽くドアを叩き、中に入っていった。カートの横を通り過ぎるとき、温かい食べ物の不快な匂いがした。彼女はすれちがう看護婦には見向きもせずに廊下を急いで歩き、子供の病室のドアを押した。

　ハワードは手を後ろに組んで、窓の前に立っていた。彼女が部屋に入ると、彼は振り返った。

　「具合はどう？」と彼女は訊いた。彼女はベッドに行った。ハンドバッグをナイト・スタンドのわきの床に落とした。ずいぶん長い間ここを離れていたような気がした。彼女は子供の顔に手を触れた。「ねえどうな

"Dr. Francis was here a little while ago," Howard said. She looked at him closely and thought his shoulders ❶were bunched a little.

"I thought he wasn't coming until eight o'clock this morning," she said quickly.

"There was another doctor with him. A ❷neurologist."

"A neurologist," she said.

Howard nodded. His shoulders were bunching, she could see that. "What'd they say, Howard? For Christ's sake, what'd they say? What is it?"

"They said they're going to take him down and run more tests on him, Ann. They think they're going to operate, honey. Honey, they *are* going to operate. They can't figure out why he won't wake up. It's more than just shock or concussion, ❸they know that much now. It's in his skull, the fracture, it has something, something to do with that, they think. So they're going to operate. I tried to call you, but I guess you'd already left the house."

"Oh, God," she said. "Oh, please, Howard, please," she said, taking his arms.

🎧B41

"Look!" Howard said. "Scotty! Look, Ann!" He turned her toward the bed.

The boy had opened his eyes, then closed them. He opened them again now. The eyes stared straight ahead for a minute, then moved

---

❶were bunched a little: 少し丸くなっている　❷neurologist: 神経科医　❸they know that much now: そこまではわかってきた

の？」

「ちょっと前にフランシス先生がここに来た」とハワードは言った。彼女は夫の顔をまじまじと見た。彼の肩がこわばって少し丸くなっているように感じられた。

「八時にならないとみえないっていう話だったじゃない？」と彼女はすかさず言った。

「もう一人別の医者も一緒だった。神経科医だ」

「神経科医」と彼女は言った。

ハワードは肯いた。彼の肩は丸まっている、と彼女はあらためて思った。「それで、何だって？　ねえ、ちゃんと言って、それでどうだったの？　なんですって？」

「また下に連れていって、もっと検査をするんだそうだ。手術することになりそうだって、ハニー、手術するんだそうだ。どうして目が覚めないのか、彼らにもわからないんだ。ショックとか脳しんとうとかいう以上に何かあるらしい。それがわかってきたんだ。頭蓋骨の関係とか、そのひびとか、そういうことが何か原因しているんじゃないかって、彼らは言うんだ。だから手術をするんだ。君に電話をしてはみたんだが、もう出たあとらしかった」

「ああ神様」と彼女は言った。「ねえハワード、ねえ、どうしよう？」彼女はそう言って、夫の腕を取った。

「おい！」とハワードは言った。「スコッティー！　ねえ、ほら見てごらん、アン！」彼は妻をベッドの方に向けた。

少年は目を開け、そしてまた閉じた。そして彼はまた目を開けていた。その目はしばらくの間じっとまっすぐ前方を見ていたが、視線はや

slowly in his head until they rested on Howard and Ann, then traveled away again.

"Scotty," his mother said, moving to the bed.

"Hey, Scott," his father said. "Hey, son."

They leaned over the bed. Howard took the child's hand in his hands and began to pat and squeeze the hand. Ann bent over the boy and kissed his forehead again and again. She put her hands on either side of his face. "Scotty, honey, it's Mommy and Daddy," she said. "Scotty?"

The boy looked at them, but without any sign of recognition. Then his mouth opened, his eyes ❶scrunched closed, and he ❷howled until he had no more air in his lungs. His face seemed to relax and soften then. His lips parted as his last breath was puffed through his throat and exhaled gently through the clenched teeth.

🎧 B42

The doctors called it a hidden ❸occlusion and said it was a one-in-a-million circumstance. Maybe if it could have been detected somehow and surgery undertaken immediately, they could have saved him. But more than likely not. In any case, what would they have been looking for? Nothing had shown up in the tests or in the X-rays.

Dr. Francis was ❹shaken. "I can't tell you how badly I feel. I'm so very sorry, I can't tell you," he said as he led them into the doctors'

---

❶scrunched closed: ぎゅっと閉じられた　★scrunchは「(目) を細める」。　❷howled: 大声をあげた　❸occlusion: 閉塞　❹shaken: 動揺して

がてぐるりと回ってハワードとアンの上に留まり、そしてまたゆっくり
と離れていった。

「スコッティー」と母親は言って、ベッドに行った。

「おい、スコット」と父親は言った。「おい、どうした？」

二人はベッドの上にかがみこんだ。ハワードは子供の手を取って、ぽ
んぽん叩いたり握ったりしはじめた。アンは子供の上に身をかがめ、お
でこに何度も何度もキスした。彼女はその両頬に手を当てた。「ねえス
コッティー、お母さんとお父さんよ」と彼女は言った。「ねえスコッ
ティー」

少年は二人を見た。でもよくわかっていないようだった。それから口
が開いた。目はぎゅっと思い切り閉じられた。そして肺の中の空気が尽
きるまで、彼は唸り声をあげた。それで彼はリラックスして、力が抜け
たように見えた。末期の息が喉を抜け、ぎゅっと嚙みしめられた歯のす
きまから安らかに出ていくとき、子供の唇は軽く開かれていた。

医師たちはそれを不可視閉塞と呼んだ。百万に一つの症例なのだと彼
らは言った。あるいはそれが何とかわかっていたら、そしてその場です
ぐ外科手術を行っていたなら、命を救うこともできたかもしれませんで
した。でもそれもおそらく難しかったでしょう。とにかく私たちには知
りようもなかったんです。検査でも、レントゲン撮影でも、不審な点は
何も出てこなかったんです。

フランシス医師はがっくりしていた。「本当にお気の毒です。申し訳
なく思っています。何とも申し上げる言葉もありません」彼はそう言っ

lounge. There was a doctor sitting in a chair with his legs hooked over the back of another chair, watching an early-morning TV show. He was wearing a green ❶delivery-room outfit, loose green pants and green blouse, and a green cap that covered his hair. He looked at Howard and Ann and then looked at Dr. Francis. He got to his feet and turned off the set and went out of the room. Dr. Francis guided Ann to the sofa, sat down beside her, and began to talk in a low, consoling voice. At one point, he leaned over and embraced her. She could feel his chest rising and falling evenly against her shoulder. She kept her eyes open and let him hold her. Howard went into the bathroom, but he left the door open. After a violent ❷fit of weeping, he ran water and washed his face. Then he came out and sat down at the little table that held a telephone. He looked at the telephone as though deciding what to do first. He made some calls. After a time, Dr. Francis used the telephone.

"Is there anything else I can do for the moment?" he asked them.

Howard shook his head. Ann stared at Dr. Francis as if unable to comprehend his words.

∩ B43

The doctor walked them to the hospital's front door. People were entering and leaving the hospital. It was eleven o'clock in the morning. Ann was aware of how slowly, almost reluctantly, she moved her feet. It seemed to her that Dr. Francis was making them leave when she felt they should stay, when it would be more the right

❶delivery-room: 分娩室　❷fit: 発作

て、医師用のラウンジに二人を連れていった。そこでは医者が一人、椅子に腰掛けて前の椅子の背もたれに足をかけ、早朝のテレビ番組を見ていた。彼は分娩室用の服を着ていた。ぶかっとしたグリーンのズボンにグリーンの上着、髪を包むグリーンのキャップ。彼はハワードとアンを見て、それからフランシス医師を見た。彼は椅子から立ち上がってテレビのスイッチを切り、部屋を出ていった。フランシス医師はアンをソファーに座らせ、その隣に座った。そして低い、慰めるような声で話し始めた。途中で身を乗り出して、彼女の体を抱いた。彼女は医者の胸が自分の肩の上で規則的に上下するのを感じることができた。彼女はしっかりと目をあけたまま、彼にじっと抱かれていた。ハワードは部屋のドアを開けたまま洗面所に行った。激しい発作に襲われたようにひとしきり涙を流したあとで、彼は水道をひねり、顔を洗った。それから彼は電話が置かれた小さなテーブルの前に腰を下ろした。さてまず何をすればいいものかと考えるように、彼はじっと電話を見た。彼は何本か電話をかけた。ちょっとあとで、フランシス医師もその電話を使った。

「何か私にお役に立てることはありますでしょうか？」と彼は二人に尋ねた。

ハワードは首を振った。アンはじっと医者を見た。この人の言っていることはまったく理解できないといった目で。

医者は二人を病院の玄関まで送った。人々は病院に入ったり、病院から出ていったりしていた。午前十一時だった。アンは自分が嫌々といってもいいくらいゆっくりと歩を運んでいることに気がついた。フランシス医師は私たちが残っていなくてはならないときに、私たちを帰らせようとしているんだ、彼女にはそう思えた。そう、私たちは今こそあそこ

thing to do to stay. She gazed out into the parking lot and then turned around and looked back at the front of the hospital. She began shaking her head. "No, no," she said. "I can't leave him here, no." She heard herself say that and thought how unfair it was that the only words that came out were the sort of words used on TV shows where people were stunned by violent or sudden deaths. She wanted her words to be her own. "No," she said, and for some reason the memory of the Negro woman's head ❶lolling on the woman's shoulder came to her. "No," she said again.

🎧 **B44**

"I'll be talking to you later in the day," the doctor was saying to Howard. "There are still some things that have to be done, things that have to be cleared up to our satisfaction. Some things that need explaining. "

"An ❷autopsy," Howard said.

Dr. Francis nodded.

"I understand," Howard said. Then he said, "Oh, Jesus. No, I don't understand, doctor. I can't, I can't. I just can't."

🎧 **B45**

Dr. Francis put his arm around Howard's shoulders. "I'm sorry. God, how I'm sorry." He let go of Howard's shoulders and held out his hand. Howard looked at the hand, and then he took it. Dr. Francis put his arms around Ann once more. He seemed full of some goodness she didn't understand. She let her head rest on his

❶loll(ing) on . . .: ～にぐったりと寄りかかる　❷autopsy: (検死) 解剖

に残っているべきなのに。彼女は駐車場に目をやり、それから振り返って、病院の玄関を見やった。彼女は頭を振りはじめた。「そんなことできない」と彼女は言った。「駄目よ。あの子をここに残してはいけない」彼女は自分がそう言う声を聞いた。そしてなんてひどい話だろう、と彼女は思った。自分の口から唯一出てくる言葉がこんなテレビ・ドラマみたいな言葉だなんて。殺されたか急死した人の前で、みんな茫然としてこういう陳腐きわまりない台詞を口ばしるのよね。彼女は自分自身の言葉が欲しかった。「駄目」と彼女は言った。そしてわけもなくあの黒人の女の記憶が蘇ってきた。頭をだらりと横に倒していたあの女。「駄目」と彼女は繰り返した。

「また後ほどゆっくりお話しします」と医師はハワードに言った。「まだやるべきことが残っているのです。納得がいくように、きちんと調べあげたいのです。どうしてこうなったか、その理由を解明する必要があるんです」

「検死解剖ですか？」とハワードは訊いた。

フランシス医師は肯いた。

「結構です」とハワードは言った。それから言いなおした。「いや、駄目だ、先生。それはできない。そんなこと私には承服できませんよ。そんなの駄目です。嫌だ」

フランシス医師は彼の肩に手を回した。「お気の毒です。本当に、お気の毒です」彼はハワードの肩から手を離し、それをさしだした。ハワードは相手の手を見て、それを握った。フランシス医師はまたアンの体に手を回した。この男はアンには理解することのできない善意に満ちているように思えた。彼女はなされるがままに医者の肩に頭をもたせか

shoulder, but her eyes stayed open. She kept looking at the hospital. As they drove out of the parking lot, she looked back at the hospital.

🎧 B46

At home, she sat on the sofa with her hands in her coat pockets. Howard closed the door to the child's room. He got the coffee-maker going and then he found an empty box. He had thought to pick up some of the child's things that were scattered around the living room. But instead he sat down beside her on the sofa, pushed the box to one side, and leaned forward, arms between his knees. He began to weep. She pulled his head over into her lap and patted his shoulder. "He's gone," she said. She kept patting his shoulder. Over his sobs, she could hear the coffee-maker hissing in the kitchen. "There, there," she said tenderly. "Howard, he's gone. He's gone and now we'll have to get used to that. To being alone."

🎧 B47

In a little while, Howard got up and began moving aimlessly around the room with the box, not putting anything into it, but collecting some things together on the floor at one end of the sofa. She continued to sit with her hands in her coat pockets. Howard put the box down and brought coffee into the living room. Later, Ann made calls to relatives. After each call had been placed and ❶the party had answered, Ann would ❷blurt out a few words and

❶the party: 相手　❷blurt out . . .: 〜を口走る

けていたが、それでも目だけはじっと見開いていた。彼女は病院を見ていた。車に乗って駐車場を出ていくときも、彼女は振り返って病院を見ていた。

　家に戻ると、彼女はコートのポケットに両手を入れたままソファーに座った。ハワードは子供部屋のドアを閉めた。彼はコーヒーメーカーのスイッチを入れ、それから空っぽの箱をみつけた。居間に散らばった子供のものを集めてそこに詰めるつもりだったが、でも思い直して、妻の隣に腰を下ろした。箱を脇に押しやり、身を前にかがめ、膝の間に両腕をはさんだ。彼は泣き始めた。彼女は夫の頭を膝の上に載せ、肩をやさしく叩いた。「あの子は死んだのよ」と彼女は言った。彼女は夫の肩を叩き続けていた。彼のすすり泣きにかぶさるように、キッチンのコーヒーメーカーが立てるしゅうぅっという音が聞こえた。「ねえ、ほら、ハワード」と彼女は優しく言った。「あの子死んじゃったのよ、もう。私たちそれに慣れなくちゃならないのよ。私たち、私たちだけなのよ」
　少したってから、ハワードは立ち上がって、箱を手にあてもなく部屋の中を歩きまわった。箱に何を入れるでもないが、それでもいくつかの品物を集めてソファーの脇の床の上にまとめて置いた。彼女は相変わらずコートのポケットに手をつっこんだままソファーに座っていた。ハワードは箱を下に置き、コーヒーを運んできた。そのあとでアンは親戚に電話をかけた。それぞれの電話の回線が繋がり、相手が出てくると、アンはいつもふたことみこと口にして、そしてほんの少しのあいだ泣い

cry for a minute. Then she would quietly explain, in a ❶measured voice, what had happened and tell them about arrangements. Howard took the box out to the garage, where he saw the child's bicycle. He dropped the box and sat down on the pavement beside the bicycle. He took hold of the bicycle awkwardly so that it leaned against his chest. He held it, the rubber pedal sticking into his chest. He gave the wheel a turn.

🎧 **B48**

Ann hung up the telephone after talking to her sister. She was looking up another number when the telephone rang. She picked it up on the first ring.

"Hello," she said, and she heard something in the background, a humming noise. "Hello!" she said. "For God's sake," she said. "Who is this? What is it you want?"

"Your Scotty, I got him ready for you," the man's voice said. "Did you forget him?"

"You evil bastard!" she shouted into the receiver. "How can you do this, you evil son of a bitch?"

"Scotty," the man said. "Have you forgotten about Scotty?" Then the man hung up on her.

Howard heard the shouting and came in to find her with her head on her arms over the table, weeping. He picked up the receiver and listened to the dial tone.

❶ measured: 落ち着いた

た。それから彼女は抑制された声で一部始終を話し、これからの段取り
について語った。ハワードは箱を持ってガレージに行った。そこには子
供の自転車があった。彼は箱を下に落とし、自転車のわきの舗道に腰を
下ろした。彼は自転車をぎこちなく摑み、それは彼の胸に倒れかかっ
た。彼はそれを支えた。ゴムのペダルが彼の胸に突きたてられた。彼は
車輪をくるくると回した。

　姉と話したあとで、彼女は受話器を置いた。次の電話番号を探してい
るときに電話のベルが鳴った。最初のベルで彼女は受話器を取った。

　「もしもし」と彼女は言った。電話の向こうの背後にぶううんという
物音が聞こえた。「もしもし！」と彼女は言った。「ねえ、いったい何な
の？　お願い。何が望みなの？　お願い。何が望みなの？　あなた誰
なんです？」

　「あんたのスコッティー。あんたのためにあの子を用意してある」と
男の声が言った。「あの子のこと忘れたのかい？」

　「悪魔！」と彼女は（受話器に）叫んだ。「この悪魔！　どうしてこんな
酷いことするの？」

　「スコッティーだよ」と男は言った。「あんたスコッティーのこと忘れ
たのかい？」そして男はがちゃんと電話を切った。

　ハワードが叫び声を聞いて戻ってきた。そして妻がテーブルにつっぷ
して、腕の中に顔を埋めているのを見た。彼は受話器を取ってみたが、
聞こえるのは信号音だけだった。

Much later, just before midnight, after they had dealt with many things, the telephone rang again.

"You answer it," she said. "Howard, it's him, I know." They were sitting at the kitchen table with coffee in front of them. Howard had a small glass of whiskey beside his cup. He answered on the third ring.

"Hello," he said. "Who is this? Hello! Hello!" The line went dead. "He hung up," Howard said. "Whoever it was."

"It was him," she said. "That bastard. I'd like to kill him," she said. "I'd like to shoot him and watch him ❶kick," she said.

"Ann, my God," he said.

"Could you hear anything?" she said. "In the background? A noise, machinery, something humming?"

"Nothing, really. Nothing like that," he said. "There wasn't much time. I think there was some radio music. Yes, there was a radio going, that's all I could tell. I don't know what in God's name is going on," he said.

She shook her head. "If I could, could get my hands on him." It came to her then. She knew who it was. Scotty, the cake, the telephone number. She pushed the chair away from the table and got up. "Drive me down to the shopping center," she said. "Howard."

❶kick: 足をばたつかせる

その日も遅くなって、いろんな雑用を済ませた後に、また電話のベル
が鳴った。真夜中近くだった。

　「あなた出てよ、ハワード」と彼女は言った。「あいつよ。私にはわか
るの」二人はコーヒーカップを前にキッチンのテーブルに座っていた。
ハワードはカップの隣にウィスキーを入れた小さなグラスを置いてい
た。彼は三回めのベルで受話器を取った。

　「もしもし」と彼は言った。「どなた？　もしもし！　もしもし！」電
話が切れた。「切れたよ」とハワードは言った。「誰だか知らんが」

　「あいつよ」と彼女は言った。「あん畜生。殺してやりたい」と彼女は
言った。「銃で撃って、のたうちまわるところを見たい」と彼女は言っ
た。

　「よすんだ、アン」と彼は言った。

　「何か聞こえなかった？」と彼女は訊いた。「後ろの方で？　騒音と
か、機械音とか、そういうもの。ぶうんというような音」

　「いや、聞こえなかったと思うな。そういうのは聞こえなかったと思
う」と彼は言った。「時間も短かったしね。ラジオの音楽が聞こえたよ
うな気がするけれど。うん、そうだ、ラジオが鳴っていた。思い出せる
のはそれくらいだよ。まったく、いったい全体何がどうなってるんだ
い？」と彼は言った。

　彼女は首を振った。「そいつを捕まえることさえできたら」そのとき、
彼女ははっと思いあたった。それが誰なのか、彼女にはわかった。ス
コッティー、ケーキ、電話番号も教えた。彼女はさっと椅子を引いて立
ち上がった。「車でショッピング・センターに連れていって」と彼女は
言った。「ねえハワード」

"What are you saying?"

"The shopping center. I know who it is who's calling. I know who it is. It's the baker, the son-of-a-bitching baker, Howard. I had him bake a cake for Scotty's birthday. That's who's calling. That's who has the number and keeps calling us. To harass us about that cake. The baker, that bastard."

∩ B51

They drove down to the shopping center. The sky was clear and stars were out. It was cold, and they ran the heater in the car. They parked in front of the bakery. All of the shops and stores were closed, but there were cars at the far end of the lot in front of the movie theater. The bakery windows were dark, but when they looked through the glass they could see a light in the back room and, now and then, a big man in an apron moving in and out of the white, ❶even light. Through the glass, she could see the display cases and some little tables with chairs. She tried the door. She rapped on the glass. But if the baker heard them, he gave no sign. He didn't look in their direction.

∩ B52

They drove around behind the bakery and parked. They got out of the car. There was a lighted window too high up for them to see inside. A sign near the back door said THE PANTRY BAKERY, SPECIAL ORDERS. She could hear faintly a radio playing inside and some-

---

❶even: 均質な

「何を言ってるんだい？」

「ショッピング・センターよ。電話をかけてる相手がわかったのよ。誰だか知ってるの。パン屋よ、あん畜生がかけてるのよ。あいつにスコッティーのバースデイ・ケーキを焼かせたのよ。そいつが電話をかけてきてるの。電話番号を知ってて、それで電話をかけてきてるのよ。ケーキのことで、私たちにいやがらせしてるのよ。あのパン屋、畜生め」

　二人は車でショッピング・センターに行った。空はくっきりと晴れて、星が出ていた。寒かったので、車のヒーターを入れた。二人はパン屋の前で車を停めた。ショッピング・センターの店はみんな閉まっていた。しかし映画館の前の駐車場の隅には何台か車が停めてあった。パン屋のウィンドウは暗かったが、じっとガラスの中を覗き込むと奥の部屋に明かりが灯っているのが見えた。エプロン姿の大柄な男が白いのっぺりとした光の中を出たり入ったりしているのも見えた。ガラスの向こうに、彼女はディスプレイ・ケースや、いくつかの小さなテーブルと椅子を見ることができた。彼女はドアを引っぱってみた。ウィンドウのガラスをこんこんこんと叩いた。しかし、もしその音がパン屋の耳に届いたとしても、彼はそんなそぶりは見せなかった。彼はこちらを向きもしなかった。

　彼らはパン屋の裏手に回って車を下りた。明かりの灯った窓は高すぎて、その中を覗くことはできなかった。裏口のわきには「各種パン洋菓子、特別注文に応じます」という看板が出ていた。中からラジオの音が微かに聞こえた。何かがぎいっと軋む音も聞こえた。オーヴンの扉を開

thing creak—an oven door as it was pulled down? She knocked on the door and waited. Then she knocked again, louder. The radio was turned down and there was a scraping sound now, the distinct sound of something, a drawer, being pulled open and then closed.

🎧 **B53**

Someone unlocked the door and opened it. The baker stood in the light and peered out at them. "I'm closed for business," he said. "What do you want at this hour? It's midnight. Are you drunk or something?"

She stepped into the light that fell through the open door. He blinked his heavy eyelids as he recognized her. "It's you," he said.

"It's me," she said. "Scotty's mother. This is Scotty's father. We'd like to come in."

The baker said, "I'm busy now. I have work to do."

She had stepped inside the doorway anyway. Howard came in behind her. The baker moved back. "It smells like a bakery in here. Doesn't it smell like a bakery in here, Howard?"

🎧 **B54**

"What do you want?" the baker said. "Maybe you want your cake? That's it, you decided you want your cake. You ordered a cake, didn't you?"

"You're pretty smart for a baker," she said. "Howard, this is the man who's been calling us." She clenched her fists. She stared at him fiercely. There was a deep burning inside her, an anger that

ける音なのだろうか？　彼女はドアをノックして、待った。それからもう一度、もっと強くどんどんとノックした。ラジオの音量が下がり、何かをこするような音が聞こえた。間違いなく何かが（たとえば引き出しが）引き開けられ、そして閉められる音だった。

　鍵が外され、ドアが開いた。光の中にパン屋の主人が立って、顔をつきだすようにして二人を凝視した。「店は閉まったよ」と彼は言った。「こんな時間に何の御用かな？　真夜中だよ。あんたら酔っぱらってるんじゃないのかい？」

　彼女は開いたドアからこぼれる光の中に足を踏み入れた。パン屋は彼女が誰かを知って、もったりとしたまつげをしばたたかせた。「あんたか」と彼は言った。

　「私よ」と彼女は言った。「スコッティーの母です。こちらはスコッティーの父親。入っていいかしら？」

　パン屋は言った。「あたしは忙しいんだよ。仕事がいっぱいあるんだ」

　彼女は構わず中に入った。ハワードはその後から入ってきた。パン屋は後ろに身を引いた。「パン屋の匂いがするわ。ねえハワード、パン屋の匂いがすると思わない？」

　「何の用だね、いったい？」とパン屋は言った。「御注文のケーキが欲しいのかね。なるほどね、やっとその気になったのかい。だって、あんたがケーキを注文したんだものな？」

　「あなた頭が働くわね。パン屋にしとくのは惜しいわ」と彼女は言った。「ねえハワード、こちらがずっと電話をかけてきた方」彼女はこぶしをぎゅっと握りしめた。そしてぎらぎらとした目で男を睨んだ。彼女の体の奥で何かが燃えていた。その怒りが彼女に、自分の体を実際以上

made her feel larger than herself, larger than either of these men.

🎧 B55

"Just a minute here," the baker said. "You want to pick up your three-day-old cake? That it? I don't want to argue with you, lady. There it sits over there, getting ❶stale. I'll give it to you for half of what I ❷quoted you. No. You want it? You can have it. It's no good to me, no good to anyone now. It cost me time and money to make that cake. If you want it, okay, if you don't, that's okay, too. I have to get back to work." He looked at them and rolled his tongue behind his teeth.

"More cakes," she said. She knew she was in control of it, of what was increasing in her. She was calm.

🎧 B56

"Lady, I work sixteen hours a day in this place to earn a living," the baker said. He wiped his hands on his apron. "I work night and day in here, trying to ❸make ends meet." A look crossed Ann's face that made the baker move back and say, "No trouble, now." He reached to the counter and picked up a rolling pin with his right hand and began to tap it against the palm of his other hand. "You want the cake or not? I have to get back to work. Bakers work at night," he said again. His eyes were small, mean-looking, she thought, nearly lost in the ❹bristly flesh around his cheeks. His neck was thick with fat.

"I know bakers work at night," Ann said. "They make phone calls

---

❶stale: 新鮮でない　❷quote(d): (価格・費用など) を提示する、見積もる　❸make ends meet: やりくりしていく、食べていく　❹bristly: 剛毛の多い

に大きく感じさせた。彼女は二人の男のどちらより大きく感じた。

「ちょっと待ちなよ」とパン屋は言った。「あんたの注文した三日前の
ケーキを持っていくかい?　それでいいのかい?　ごたごたは御免だ
よ、奥さん。まだケーキはそこに置いてあるよ。腐りかけてるけどな。
正価の半分の値段であんたに譲ろう。いいや、欲しきゃただで持って
いっていいよ。あたしが持ってても仕方ないものな。誰が持ってたって
今更仕方ないけどね。言っとくが、そのケーキ作るのには時間もかかっ
たし、金もかかった。でも欲しければ持っていきなよ。いらないんなら
置いていきゃいい。どっちでも構わん。とにかくあたしは仕事に戻る
よ」彼は二人を見て、歯の奥で舌を丸めた。

「もっとケーキを焼いてちょうだい」彼女は言った。彼女は自分がそれ
をコントロールしていることを知っていた。自分の中にわきあがってく
るものを、彼女はコントロールすることができた。彼女は冷静だった。

「なあ奥さん、あたしはおまんま食うために一日十六時間ここで働い
てるんだよ」とパン屋は言った。彼は両手をエプロンで拭いた。「ここ
で昼といわず夜といわず働いている。日々の銭を稼ぐためにね」アンの
顔をある表情がさっとよぎった。パン屋はそれを見て後ずさりして、
言った。「面倒は嫌だぜ」彼は手をのばしてカウンターの上ののし棒を
右手に摑み、もう一方の手のひらをぱんぱんと叩いた。「ケーキが欲し
いの、欲しくないの?　あたしは仕事をしなきゃならないんだよ。パン
屋は夜中に働くんだ」と彼は繰り返して言った。彼の目は小さく、狡そ
うな光を放っていた。目は今にも頰のまわりの毛の生えた肉の中に沈み
こんでしまいそうだ、と彼女は思った。彼の首は脂肪でむくんでいた。

「パン屋が夜中に働くことは知ってるわ」とアンは言った。「そして夜

at night, too. You bastard," she said.

The baker continued to tap the rolling pin against his hand. He glanced at Howard. "Careful, careful," he said to Howard.

🎧**B57**

"My son's dead," she said ❶with a cold, even finality. "He was hit by a car Monday morning. We've been waiting with him until he died. But, of course, you couldn't be expected to know that, could you? Bakers can't know everything—can they, Mr Baker? But he's dead. He's dead, you bastard!" Just as suddenly ❷as it had welled in her, the anger ❸dwindled, gave way to something else, a dizzy feeling of nausea. She leaned against the wooden table that was sprinkled with flour, put her hands over her face, and began to cry, her shoulders rocking back and forth. "It isn't fair," she said. "It isn't, isn't fair."

Howard put his hand at ❹the small of her back and looked at the baker. "Shame on you," Howard said to him. "Shame."

🎧**B58**

The baker put the rolling pin back on the counter. He undid his apron and threw it on the counter. He looked at them, and then he shook his head slowly. He pulled a chair out from under the card table that held papers and receipts, an adding machine, and a telephone directory. "Please sit down," he said. "Let me get you a chair," he said to Howard. "Sit down now, please." The baker went into the front of the shop and returned with two little wrought-

---

❶with a cold, even finality: 冷たい、平板で決定的な口調で ❷as it had welled in her: それが湧きあがってきた時と同じように ❸dwindled: すうっと消えていった ❹the small of her back: 腰のくびれ

A SMALL, GOOD THING by Raymond Carver

中に電話もかけるのよ。こん畜生」と彼女は言った。

　パン屋はのし棒をぴしゃぴしゃと叩き続けていた。彼はちらっとハワードの方を見た。「気をつけろよ」と彼はハワードに向かって言った。

　「子供は死にました」と彼女は冷たい平板な声で言った。「月曜の朝に車にはねられたんです。死ぬまで、私たち二人はずっと子供に付き添っていました。でももちろん、あなたにはそんなことわかりっこないわね。パン屋にはなにもかもがわかるってわけもないし。そうよね、パン屋さん？　でもあの子は死んだの。死んだのよ、こん畜生！」その怒りは、それが湧きあがってきた時と同じように、だしぬけにすうっと消えていって、何かもっと別のものに姿を変えてしまった。くらくらとするむかつきのようなものに。彼女は小麦粉の散った木のテーブルに寄り掛かり、両手で顔を覆った。そして泣き始めた。肩が大きく前後に揺れた。「こんなのあんまりよ」と彼女は言った。「こんなの、こんなのって、あんまりだわ」

　ハワードは妻の腰のくびれに手を置いた。そしてパン屋を見た。「恥を知れ」とハワードはパン屋に向かって言った。「恥を知れ」

　パン屋はのし棒をカウンターに戻した。そしてエプロンを取り、カウンターの上に投げた。彼は二人を見て、それからゆっくりと首を振った。彼はカード・テーブルの椅子を引いた。テーブルの上には書類や領収書や計算機や電話帳なんかが載っていた。「お座りなさい」と彼は言った。「今椅子を持ってきます」と彼はハワードに向かって言った。「どうぞ、座って」と彼はハワードに言った。「どうか座って下さい」パン屋は店頭に行って、小さな錬鉄製の椅子を二つ持って戻ってきた。

iron chairs. "Please sit down, you people."

Ann wiped her eyes and looked at the baker. "I wanted to kill you," she said. "I wanted you dead."

∩B59

The baker had cleared a space for them at the table. He shoved the adding machine to one side, along with the stacks of notepaper and receipts. He pushed the telephone directory onto the floor, where it landed ❶with a thud. Howard and Ann sat down and pulled their chairs up to the table. The baker sat down, too.

∩B60

"Let me say how sorry I am," the baker said, putting his elbows on the table. "God alone knows how sorry. Listen to me. I'm just a baker. I don't claim to be anything else. Maybe once, maybe years ago, I was a different kind of human being. I've forgotten, I don't know for sure. But I'm not any longer, if I ever was. Now I'm just a baker. That don't excuse my doing what I did, I know. But I'm deeply sorry. I'm sorry for your son, and sorry for my part in this," the baker said. He spread his hands out on the table and turned them over to reveal his palms. "I don't have any children myself, so I can only imagine what you must be feeling. All I can say to you now is that I'm sorry. Forgive me, if you can," the baker said. "I'm not an evil man, I don't think. Not evil, like you said on the phone. You got to understand ❷what it comes down to is I don't know how to act anymore, it would seem. Please," the man said, "let me

---

❶with a thud: どさっという音を立てて   ❷what it comes down to is . . .: つまるところは〜

「どうか、腰かけて下さい」

　アンは涙を拭き、パン屋を見た。「あなたを殺してやりたかった」と彼女は言った。「死なせてやりたかった」

　パン屋は二人のためにテーブルの上をかたづけた。計算機を隅の方に押しやり、メモ用紙や領収書の束の脇に並べた。電話帳は床の上に払い落とした。それはどさっという音を立てて落ちた。ハワードとアンは腰を下ろし、椅子を前に引いた。パン屋も座った。

　「本当にお気の毒です」とパン屋は言った。彼はテーブルの上に両肘をついた。「なんとも言いようがないほど、お気の毒に思っております。聞いて下さい。あたしはただのつまらんパン屋です。それ以上の何者でもない。昔は、何年か前は、たぶんあたしもこんなじゃなかった。でも昔のことが思い出せないんです。あたしが一人のちゃんとした人間だったときもあったはずなのに、それが思い出せんのです。今のあたしはただのパンを焼くパン屋、それだけです。もちろんそれで、あたしのやったことが許してもらえるとは思っちゃいません。でも心から済まなく思っています。あんたのお子さんのことはお気の毒だった。そしてあたしのやったことはまったくひどいことだった」とパン屋は言った。彼は両手をテーブルの上で広げ、それからひっくり返して手のひらを見せた。「あたしには子供がおりません。だからお気持ちはただ想像するしかない。申し訳ないという以外に何とも言いようがない。もし許してもらえるものなら、許して下さい」とパン屋は言った。「あたしは邪悪な人間じゃありません。そう思っとります。あたしは奥さんが電話で言われたような邪悪な人間じゃありません。つまるところ、あたしは人間としてのまっとうな生き方を見うしなってしまったんです。そのことをわ

ask you if you can ❶find it in your hearts to forgive me?"

🎧 B61

It was warm inside the bakery. Howard stood up from the table and took off his coat. He helped Ann from her coat. The baker looked at them for a minute and then nodded and got up from the table. He went to the oven and turned off some switches. He found cups and poured coffee from an electric coffee-maker. He put a carton of cream on the table, and a bowl of sugar.

"You probably need to eat something," the baker said. "I hope you'll eat some of my hot rolls. You have to eat and keep going. Eating is a small, good thing in a time like this," he said.

🎧 B62

He served them warm cinnamon rolls just out of the oven, the icing still runny. He put butter on the table and knives to spread the butter. Then the baker sat down at the table with them. He waited. He waited until they each took a roll from the platter and began to eat. "It's good to eat something," he said, watching them. "There's more. Eat up. Eat all you want. There's all the rolls in the world in here."

🎧 B63

They ate rolls and drank coffee. Ann was suddenly hungry, and the rolls were warm and sweet. She ate three of them, which pleased the baker. Then he began to talk. They listened carefully. Although they were tired and in anguish, they listened to what the

❶ find it in your hearts to . . .: 〜する気になる

かって下さい。お願いです」とその男は言った。「聞かせて下さい。奥さんにあたしを許して下さるお心持ちがあるかどうか?」

　パン屋の店内は温かかった。ハワードは立ち上がってコートを脱いだ。そしてアンのコートも脱がせた。パン屋は二人をちょっと見て、それから肯いて席を立った。それからオーヴンのところに行っていくつかのスイッチを切った。カップをみつけて、電気コーヒーメーカーからコーヒーを注いだ。紙の箱に入ったクリームと砂糖壺をテーブルに置いた。

　「何か召し上がらなくちゃいけませんよ」とパン屋は言った。「よかったら、あたしが焼いた温かいロールパンを食べて下さい。ちゃんと食べて、頑張って生きていかなきゃならんのだから。こんなときには、ものを食べることです。それはささやかなことですが、助けになります」と彼は言った。

　彼はオーヴンから出したばかりの、まだ砂糖が固まっていない温かいシナモン・ロールを出した。彼はバターとバター・ナイフをテーブルの上に置いた。パン屋は二人と一緒にテーブルについた。彼は待った。彼は二人がそれぞれに大皿からひとつずつパンを取って口に運ぶのを待った。「何かを食べるって、いいことなんです」と彼は二人を見ながら言った。「もっと沢山あります。好きなだけ食べて下さい。世界じゅうのロールパンを集めたくらい、ここにはいっぱいあるんです」

　二人はロールパンを食べ、コーヒーを飲んだ。アンは突然空腹を感じた。ロールパンは温かく、甘かった。彼女は三個食べた。パン屋はそれを見て喜んだ。それから彼は話し始めた。彼らは注意深く耳を傾けた。二人は疲れきって、深い苦悩の中にいたが、それでもパン屋が打ちあけ

baker had to say. They nodded when the baker began to speak of loneliness, and of the sense of doubt and limitation that had come to him in his middle years. He told them what it was like to be childless all these years. To repeat the days with the ovens endlessly full and endlessly empty. The party food, the celebrations he'd worked over. Icing knuckle-deep. The tiny wedding couples stuck into cakes. Hundreds of them, no, thousands by now. Birthdays. Just imagine all those candles burning. He had a necessary trade. He was a baker. He was glad he wasn't a florist. It was better to be feeding people. This was a better smell anytime than flowers.

🎧 B64

"Smell this," the baker said, breaking open a dark loaf. "It's a heavy bread, but rich." They smelled it, then he had them taste it. It had the taste of ❶molasses and coarse grains. They listened to him. They ate what they could. They swallowed the dark bread. It was like daylight under ❷the fluorescent trays of light. They talked on into the early morning, the high, pale cast of light in the windows, and they did not think of leaving.

---

❶molasses and coarse grains: 糖蜜とあら挽きの穀物　❷the fluorescent trays of light: 長方形のケースに収まった蛍光灯

る話にじっと耳を傾けた。パン屋が孤独について、中年期に彼を襲った疑いの念と無力感について語り始めたとき、二人は肯きながらその話を聞いた。この歳までずっと子供も持たずに生きてくるというのがどれほど寂しいものか、彼は二人に語った。オーヴンをいっぱいにしてオーヴンを空っぽにしてという、ただそれだけを毎日繰り返すことが、どういうものかということを。パーティーの食事やらお祝いのケーキやらを作り続けるのがどういうものかということを。指のつけねまでどっぷりと漬かるアイシング。ケーキについた小さな飾りの新郎新婦。そういうのが何百と続くのだ。いや、今ではもう何千という数になるだろう。誕生日。それだけのキャンドルが一斉に燃えあがる様を想像してみるがいい。彼は世の中の役にたつ仕事をしているのだ。彼はパン屋なのだ。彼は花屋にならなくてよかったと思っている。花を売るよりは、人に自分の作ったものを食べてもらう方がいい。匂いだって、花よりは食べ物の方がいい。

　「匂いをかいでみて下さい」とダーク・ローフを二つに割りながらパン屋は言った。「こいつはがっしりしてるが、リッチなパンです」二人はそのパンの匂いをかぎ、パン屋にすすめられて、一くち食べてみた。糖蜜とあら挽き麦の味がした。二人は彼の話に耳を傾けた。二人は食べられる限りパンを食べた。彼らは黒パンを飲み込んだ。蛍光灯の光の下にいると、それはまるで日の光のように感じられた。彼らは夜明けまで語り続けた。太陽の白っぽい光が窓の高みに射した。でも誰も席を立とうとは思わなかった。

LEDERHOSEN
by
Haruki Murakami

レーダーホーゼン
村上春樹

　村上春樹が日本語で書き、短篇集『回転木馬のデッドヒート』（1985）に収めた短篇を、アルフレッド・バーンバウムが一部手を加えて英訳し、イギリスの文芸誌 *Granta* 42号（1992年12月刊）に発表した。ご存知の方も多いと思うが、村上春樹は、このバーンバウム・バージョンを日本語に「翻訳」して、『象の消滅　短篇選集 1980-1991』（2005）に収録している。

　村上春樹の文章について、僕が余計な口を出す必要はないと思うが、まずは、初めて出会う英語圏の作家を聴く／読むつもりで、英訳をお聴き／お読みになってみるのが面白いと思う。そういうつもりで接しても全然違和感がないか、それとも「やっぱり英米の作家とは違う」と思われるだろうか……まあたぶん、話そのものに引き込まれて、そんなことは忘れてしまうだろうが。そうやって話の面白さを十分味わったら、次は日本語原文（あるいは日本語「重訳」）を読んだときとどう印象が違うか見てみたり、村上春樹が訳している作家たち（たとえば、まさに本書に入っているオブライエンやカーヴァー）の文章と較べてみたり、いろんな形で遊べそうである。（柴田元幸）

🎧 B65

"Mother **❶**dumped my father," a friend of my wife's was saying one day, "all because of a pair of shorts."

I've got to ask. "A pair of shorts?"

"I know it sounds strange," she says, "because it is a strange story."

🎧 B66

A large woman, her height and build are almost the same as mine. She tutors electric organ, but most of her free time she divides among swimming and skiing and tennis, so she's trim and always tanned. You might call her **❷**a sports fanatic. On days off, she puts in a morning run before heading to the local pool to **❸**do laps; then at two or three in the afternoon it's tennis, followed by aerobics. **❹**Now, I like my sports, but I'm **❺**nowhere near her league.

I don't mean to suggest she's aggressive or **❻**obsessive about things. Quite the contrary, she's really rather **❼**retiring; **❽**she'd never dream of putting emotional pressure on anyone. Only, **❾**she's driven; her body—and very likely the spirit attached to that body—**❿**craves after vigorous activity, **⓫**relentless as a comet.

🎧 B67

Which may have something to do with why she's unmarried. Oh, she's **⓬**had affairs—the woman may be a little **⓭**on the large side, but she is beautiful; she's been proposed to, even agreed to

---

❶dump(ed): 〜を捨てる **❷**a sports fanatic: スポーツ・マニア **❸**do laps: ラップ・スイミングをする ★a lapで「（プールや走路の）一往復・一周」を指す。 **❹**Now, I like my sports, but . . .: そりゃあ、私だって私なりにスポーツは好きだけど **❺**nowhere near her league: 彼女の足元にも及ばない **❻**obsessive: 偏執的な、異常なまでにこだわる **❼**retiring: 引っ込みがちな **❽**she'd never dream of putting emotional pressure on anyone: 人に自分の感情を押しつけようなどとは考えたりもしない **❾**she's driven: 何かに駆られている人なのだ **❿**craves after vigorous

「うちのお母さんはお父さんを捨てたの」と妻の女友だちがある日、僕に言う。「半ズボンがその原因だった」

僕は質問しないわけにはいかない。「半ズボン？」

「妙な話に聞こえることはわかっているんだけど」と彼女は言う。「でもね、そもそもが妙な話なわけ」

彼女は女性としては大柄なほうだ。身長や体格はほとんど僕と同じくらい。仕事はエレクトーンの教師だが、自由になる時間の大半を、水泳やスキーやテニスにあてている。だから身体には無駄な贅肉はいっさいなく、いつもまんべんなく日焼けしている。スポーツ・マニアと呼んで差し支えないだろう。仕事のない日には、朝のランニングをすませてから、近くのプールに行ってひとしきりラップ・スイミングをする。午後の二時か三時になるとテニスをして、そのあとはエアロビクスという段取りである。僕だってスポーツをするのは好きだけれど、とてもそこまではできない。

彼女は攻撃的な性格でもないし、偏狭なところがあるわけでもない。というか、どちらかというとおっとりとしていて、押しつけがましいところもない。ただ彼女の身体は —— そこに付随する精神もきっと似たようなものなのだろうが —— 休むことなくせわしなく動きまわっている。それはまるでほうき星のように、静止することがない。

彼女が結婚をしないのは、そういうことと何か関係しているのかもしれない。もちろんこれまでつきあった相手は何人かいた。大柄ではあったけれど、なかなか美人だったから。求婚され、もう少しで華燭の典と

activity: 精力的で激しい活動（vigorous activity）に焦がれている（crave after . . .）　⓫relentless as a comet: ★直訳は「ほうき星のごとく執拗に」。日本語においても英語においても珍しい、村上春樹特有の比ゆ表現。　⓬had affairs: 関係を持った　⓭(be) on the large side: やや大きめの

❶take the plunge. But inevitably, ❷whenever it's gotten to the wedding stage, some problem has come up and everything falls through.

Like my wife says, "She's just unlucky."

"Well, I guess," I sympathize.

🎧B68

I'm not in total agreement with my wife on this. True, luck may rule over parts of a person's life and ❸luck may cast patches of shadow across the ground of our being, but where there's a will—❹much less a strong will to swim thirty laps or run twenty kilometers—there's a way to overcome most any trouble with whatever stepladders you have around. No, her heart was never set on marrying, is how I see it. Marriage just doesn't ❺fall within the sweep of her comet, at least not entirely.

And so she keeps on tutoring electric organ, devoting every free moment to sports, falling regularly in and out of unlucky love.

🎧B69

It's a rainy Sunday afternoon and she's come two hours earlier than expected, while my wife is still out shopping.

"Forgive me," she apologizes. "I ❻took a rain check on today's tennis, which left me two hours to spare. I'd have been bored out of my mind being alone at home, so I just thought . . . Am I interrupting anything?"

---

❶take the plunge: 結婚を決意する ❷whenever it's gotten to the wedding stage, some problem has come up and everything falls through: いざ結婚という段階になるといつも、なんらかの問題が持ち上がって、結局破綻する ❸luck may cast patches of shadow across the ground of our being: 運というものはときに、我々の存在の根底にまだらの影をおとす ❹much less: (否定語句のあとで) ましてや、なおさら ❺fall within the sweep of . . .: ～の範囲に入る ❻took a rain check: 先にのばした、また今度にした ★決まり文句。

いうところまで行ったことも何度かあった。しかしいざ結婚式が近づいてくると、必ず何か予期せぬ問題が持ち上がって、結婚は急遽中止ということになった。

「運が悪いのよ」と僕の妻は言う。

「そうらしいね」と僕もいちおう同情する。

でも僕は、必ずしも妻の意見に同意しているわけではない。たしかに運不運というのは、僕らの人生の多くの局面を左右するし、それは時として我々のまわりに黒々とした影を落とすことになる。でも僕は思うのだけれど、もしプールを30往復し、20キロを走ることができるほどの意志の力を持ち合わせているなら、たいていの障害はなんとかして乗り越えていけるものではあるまいか？　彼女は本当は結婚なんかしたくなかったのだ、というのが僕の推測である。結婚は、ほうき星としての彼女の引力圏には —— 少なくとも全面的にはということだが —— 含まれていなかったのだ。

というようなわけで、彼女はエレクトーン教室で教え、余った時間を惜しみなく運動に注ぎ込み、それほど幸運とは言えない恋に落ちたり、落ちなかったりしていた。

日曜日の雨の午後だ。彼女は予定より二時間早くうちにやってくる。妻は買い物に出ている。

「ごめんなさいね」と彼女は詫びる。「テニスをする予定だったんだけど、それがこの雨で流れて、おかげで二時間ほど余っちゃったの。家に一人でいてもつまらないし、だからちょっと早い目に来させてもらったんだけど —— ねえ、あなたのお仕事の邪魔をしちゃったかしら？」

Not at all, I say. I didn't feel quite ❶in the mood to work and was just ❷sitting around, cat on my lap, watching a video. I show her in, go to the kitchen and make coffee. Two cups, for watching the last twenty minutes of *Jaws*. Of course, we've both seen the movie before—probably more than once—so neither of us is particularly ❸riveted to the tube. But anyway, we're watching it because it's there in front of our eyes.

🎧 **B70**

It's *The End*. The credits roll up. ❹No sign of my wife. So we chat a bit. Sharks, seaside, swimming . . . still no wife. We go on talking. Now, I suppose I like the woman well enough, but after an hour of this our lack of things in common becomes obvious. In a word, she's my wife's friend, not mine.

🎧 **B71**

Short of what else to do, I'm already thinking about popping in the next video when she suddenly brings up the story of her parents' divorce. I can't ❺fathom the connection—at least to my mind, there's no link between swimming and her folks splitting up—but I guess a reason is where you find it.

🎧 **B72**

"They weren't really shorts," she says. "They were ❻lederhosen."

---

❶in the mood to . . .: 〜 する 気 に なって　　❷sit(ting) around: 何 も せ ず に ぶ ら ぶ ら 過 ご す
❸ (be) riveted to the tube: 画面 に 釘付 けに なる　　❹No sign of . . .: いっ こ う に 〜 の 兆 し が な い
❺fathom: 〜 を 推 し 測 る　　❻lederhosen: ★ ド イ ツ ・ バ イ エ ル ン 地方 の、 伝統的 な 革製 半 ズ ボ ン。
同 地方 で は、 成人 男性 が レ ー ダ ー ホ ー ゼ ン を 伝統 衣装 と し て 着用 す る 伝統 が あ り、 こ の 衣装 が 後 に
登山者 に 普及 し た。

いや、ぜんぜん、と僕は言う。あまり仕事をする気分になれなかったので、猫を膝に抱いて、のんびりビデオを見ていたところだった。僕は彼女を中に入れ、台所でコーヒーを作る。そして二人でコーヒーを飲みながら、「ジョーズ」の最後の20分を見る。もちろん僕らは二人とも、その映画を前に見ていた。たぶん二度か三度見ていたと思う。だからどちらも画面に釘付けになっていたというわけではない。とにかく目の前にたまたまその映画が映っていたから、なんとなく見ていたわけだ。

　映画が終わって、エンド・クレジットが出る。しかし妻が戻ってくる気配はない。だから僕らは適当に話をする。サメのこと、ビーチのこと、水泳のこと……それでもまだ妻は戻ってこない。だから更に話を続ける。なんというか、僕はこの女性に対して好感のようなものを持っていると思う。しかし一時間ばかり彼女と会話を続けて、その結果明らかになったのは、僕らのあいだには共通の話題と言えるようなものはとくにないという事実だった。結局のところ、彼女はうちの奥さんの友だちであって、僕の友だちではないのだ。

　ほかにやるべきことも思いつかなかったので、僕は別のビデオを機械に入れようかと考える。でもそのとき彼女が出し抜けに、両親の離婚の話を持ち出したわけだ。どうして急にそんな話になってしまったのか、僕にはぜんぜん理解できない。というのは、泳ぐことと、彼女の父母が離婚したこととのあいだには —— 少なくとも僕の思考体系の中においてはということだが —— 関連性らしきものは見いだせないからだ。でもそこにはきっと何らかの理由があったのだろう。

　「正確に言えば、それは半ズボンじゃないの」と彼女は言う。「レー

"You mean those hiking pants the Germans wear? The ones with the shoulder straps?"

"❶You got it. Father wanted a pair of lederhosen as a souvenir gift. Well, Father's pretty tall ❷for his generation. He might even look good in them, which could be why he wanted them. But can you ❸picture a Japanese wearing lederhosen? I guess ❹it takes all kinds."

🎧B73

I'm still not any ❺closer to the story. I have to ask, what were the circumstances behind her father's request—and of whom?—for these souvenir lederhosen?

"Oh, I'm sorry. I'm always telling things ❻out of order. Stop me if things don't make sense," she says.

Okay, I say.

🎧B74

"Mother's sister was living in Germany and she invited Mother for a visit. ❼Something she'd always been meaning to do. Of course, Mother can't speak German, she'd never even been abroad, but having been an English teacher for so long she'd ❽had that overseas bee in her bonnet. It'd been ❾ages since she'd seen my aunt. So Mother approached Father, How about taking ten days off and going to Germany, the two of us? Father's work couldn't allow it, and Mother ❿ended up going alone."

---

❶You got it: そのとおり ★決まり文句。 ❷for his generation: 彼の世代の人としては ❸picture: 〜を心に描く ❹it takes all kinds: 人の好みはさまざまだ、世の中にはいろいろな人がいる ❺(be) closer to the story: 話の筋が見えてくる、話の筋を理解する ❻out of order: 順番をばらばらに ❼something she'd . . .: ★この一文の訳は省略されている。 ❽had that overseas bee in her bonnet: 海外に行くことに興味はあった ★have a bee in one's bonnetは「（ある考えに）とりつかれている」。 ❾ages: ★「長い間」の意でa long time の誇張表現。 ❿end(ed) up

ダーホーゼンなわけ」

「あの、それはドイツ人がはいている、アルプス風の革ズボンのこと？　ストラップで肩にとめるようになっているやつ」

「そう、それのこと。うちのお父さんはお土産にレーダーホーゼンがほしいって言った。つまりね、うちのお父さんはそういう年代の人としては、背がけっこう高いのよ。だからレーダーホーゼンは似合ったかもしれない。だからこそそんなものを欲しがったんだと思う。でもさ、レーダーホーゼンをはいた日本人なんて想像できる？　もちろんそういうのって、人の好きずきだとは思うけど」

僕には依然として話の筋がよく見えない。だから僕は質問をしなくてはならない。いったいどのような事情で、そしていったい誰に、お父さんがレーダーホーゼンをお土産に頼むことになったのか？

「ああ、ごめんなさい。私って、いつも話の順番がごちゃごちゃになっちゃうの。だから話の筋がよくわからなくなったら、途中で遠慮なく質問してね」

そうする、と僕は言う。

「お母さんの妹がドイツに住んでいて、一度来ないかって前から誘われていたの。もちろんお母さんはドイツ語なんてしゃべれないし、生まれてから外国に行ったこともなかった。でもずっと英語の先生をしていたものだから、海外に行くことに興味はあったの。もうずいぶん長いあいだその叔母に会っていなかったしね。だからお母さんはお父さんを誘った。一緒に二人で十日ばかりドイツを旅行しないかって。でもお父さんはどうしても仕事を休むことができなかった。それでお母さんは一人でドイツに行くことになったわけ」

...ing: 結局〜するはめになる

"That's when your father asked for the lederhosen, ❶I take it?"

"Right," she says. "Mother asked what he wanted her to bring back, and Father said lederhosen."

"Okay so far."

🎧B75

Her parents were ❷reasonably close. They didn't argue until all hours of the night; her father didn't ❸storm out of the house and not come home for days ❹on end. At least not then, though apparently there had been ❺rows more than once over him and other women.

🎧B76

"Not a bad man, a hard worker, but kind of ❻a skirt chaser," she ❼tosses off matter-of-factly. No relation of hers, the way she's talking. For a second, I almost think her father is deceased. But no, I'm told, he's alive and well.

"Father was already ❽up there in years, and by then those troubles were all behind them. They seemed to be getting along just fine."

🎧B77

❾Things, however, didn't go without incident. Her mother extended the ten days in Germany to nearly a month and a half, with hardly a word back to Tokyo, and when she finally did return to Japan she stayed with another sister of hers in Osaka. ❿She never did come back home.

---

❶I take it?: ということかな？ ❷reasonably close: それなりに仲がよかった ❸storm out of the house: 怒って家を飛び出す ❹on end: 続けて、ぶっとおしで ❺rows over . . .: 〜をめぐる口論 ❻a skirt chaser: 女たらし、女癖の悪い男 ❼tosses off: あっさり淡々と言い添える ❽up there in years: もうずいぶん歳が行って ❾Things, however, didn't go without incident.: しかし、物事は無事には進まなかった ❿She never did . . .: ★この一文の訳は省略されている。

「そのときに君のお父さんは、レーダーホーゼンをお土産に買ってき
てほしいとお母さんに頼んだ。そういうことだね？」
　「そのとおり」と彼女は言う。「どんなものをお土産に買ってきてほし
いかとお母さんにきかれて、レーダーホーゼンがいいとお父さんは言っ
た」
　「そこまではわかった」
　彼女の両親はどちらかといえば仲が良い方だった。夜通し言い争いを
したりすることはなかったし、父親が荒々しく家を飛び出して、そのま
ま数日間帰ってこないというようなこともなかった。父親がよそで浮気
をして、それで家庭が不和におちいったことが、以前には幾度かあった
らしいが、今ではそういうこともなくなっていた。
　「悪い人じゃないのよ。仕事はちゃんとするし。でもね、すぐに女の
人に手を出しちゃうタイプだったわけ」、彼女はあっさりとそう言う。
まるで他人事みたいに。一瞬僕は、お父さんは既に亡くなっているのか
と思ったくらいだ。でもそうではなかった。今でも元気でぴんぴんして
る、と彼女は言う。
　「でもその頃にはお父さんも、もうすっかり落ち着いていて、面倒な
ことは起こさないようになっていた。それで、二人はけっこううまく
やっているみたいに、私の目には見えたんだけど」
　しかし話はそう簡単ではない。十日後には戻ってくる予定だったの
に、母親は結局一ヵ月半もドイツに滞在することになった。それについ
て家にほとんど一言の連絡もなかった。そしてようやく日本に帰国して
も、彼女は東京の家には戻らず、大阪にいるもう一人の妹のところに
行ってしまった。

Neither she—the daughter—nor her father could understand what was going on. Until then, when there'd been marital difficulties, her mother had always been ❶the patient one—so ❷ploddingly patient, in fact, that she sometimes wondered if the woman had no imagination; ❸family always came first, and the mother was selflessly devoted to her daughter. So when the mother didn't come around, didn't even make the effort to call, it was beyond their comprehension. They made phone calls to the aunt's house in Osaka, repeatedly, but they could hardly ❹get her to come to the phone, ❺much less admit what her intentions were.

In mid-September, two months after returning to Japan, her mother made her intentions known. One day, ❻out of the blue, she called home and told her husband, "❼You will be receiving the necessary papers for divorce. Please sign, seal, and send back to me." Would she care to explain, her husband asked, what was the reason? "I've lost all love for you—in any way, shape, or form." Oh? said her husband. Was there no room for discussion? "Sorry, none, absolutely none."

Telephone negotiations dragged on for the next two or three months, but her mother ❽did not back down an inch, and finally her father consented to the divorce. He was in no position to force

---

❶the patient one: （二者の中で）我慢強い方　★「the＋形容詞＋one」は、二者を比較する際に便利な表現。　❷ploddingly: こつこつと、地道に　❸family always came first: 家庭がいつも第一だった　★come firstは「いちばん大切である」。　❹get her to come to the phone: 彼女を電話口まで来させる　❺much less admit what her intentions were ...: ★訳文ではこの部分と続く一文（In mid-September ...）が省略されている。省略された部分は、バーンバウムが英訳した『回転木馬のデッドヒート』所収の原典では以下のようになっている。「彼女にその真意を問いただすことさえで

いったい何が起こったのか、彼女にも父親にも、さっぱりわけがわからなかった。それ以前、夫婦のあいだに不和が生じたときにも、母親はいつもただじっと苦境に耐えていた。その我慢強い様子を目にしながら、この人にはひょっとして想像力ってものがないのかしら、と彼女はよく考えたものだった。母親にとっては家庭というものがまず第一であり、何があろうとも娘を守らなくてはならなかった。だから母親が家に帰ってもこないし、電話ひとつかけてこないというようなことは、二人にとってはまさに青天の霹靂だった。二人は大阪の叔母の家に何度も電話をかけてみた。しかし母親は電話口にも出てこなかった。

　しかしある日、突然母親は自分から電話をかけてきて、夫に向かって「離婚に必要な書類を送りますから、サインして送り返してください」と言った。どういうことか説明くらいしてくれないか、と夫は言った、いったい何があったんだ？　「どんなかたちでも、どんなやり方でも、もうあなたに対して愛情が持てなくなったんです」。そこには話し合いの余地みたいなものはないのかな、と父親は尋ねた。「ありません。申しわけないとは思うけれど、もうすっかり終わったんです」

　電話での話し合いは二ヵ月か三ヵ月ずるずると続いた。しかし母親は一歩も譲らなかった。そして父親もついに折れて、離婚に合意した。父親の方としても、脛に傷があったわけだから、そう強気に出ることもで

きなかった。母親の真意が判明したのは、彼女が帰国してから二カ月ばかり経過した九月半ばのことだった」。　❻out of the blue: 突然、思いがけなく　❼You will be receiving the necessary papers for divorce. Please sign, seal, and send back to me.: ★事務的なニュアンスがひしひしと伝わってくる表現。原典『回転』は、「離婚手続きに必要な書類を送るので署名捺印の上送り返してほしい」と事務的な口調になっている。　❽did not back down an inch: 少しも後にひかなかった、一歩も譲らなかった

the issue, ❶his own track record being what it was, and anyway, he always tended to give in.

"All this came as a big shock," she tells me. "But it wasn't just the divorce. I'd imagined my parents splitting up many times, so I was already prepared for it psychologically. If the two of them had just plain divorced without all that funny business, I wouldn't have gotten so upset. The problem wasn't Mother dumping Father; Mother was dumping me, too. That's what hurt."

I nod.

🎧B81

"Up to that point, I'd always taken Mother's side, and Mother would always stand by me. And yet here was Mother throwing me out with Father, like so much garbage, and not a word of explanation. It hit me so hard, I wasn't able to forgive Mother for the longest time. I ❷wrote her who knows how many letters asking her to ❸set things straight, but she never answered my questions, never even said she wanted to see me."

🎧B82

It wasn't until three years later that she actually saw her mother. At a family funeral, ❹of all places. By then, the daughter was living on her own—she'd moved out in her sophomore year, when her parents divorced—and now she had graduated and was tutoring electric organ. Meanwhile, her mother was teaching English at a ❺prep school.

---

❶his own track record being what it was: 過去の記録が何しろああなので　❷wrote her who knows how many letters: 何通かわからないくらいたくさんお母さんに手紙を書いた　❸set things straight: 問題を解決する、物事を説明する　❹of all places: 所もあろうに、よりによって ❺prep school: 英語では名門の私立高等学校を指すが、ここでは日本式に「予備校」。

きなかった。それに父親は、ねばり強い性格の人としては知られていない。

「それは私にとっても、すごく大きなショックだった」と彼女は僕に言う。「離婚そのものがショックだったんじゃないの。両親がいつか離婚するかもしれないということは、まったく予想しないわけではなかった。だから心理的には、そういう事態に対する覚悟はある程度できていたの。もし二人がごく普通に、わけのわからない経緯抜きで、ただあっさり離婚していたとしたら、私はそれほど混乱しなかったと思う。問題はお母さんがお父さんを捨てたということじゃないのよ。彼女は私のこともひとまとめにして捨てたの。私にとってはそれがずいぶんきつかったのね」

僕は頷く。

「そういうことが起こるまでは、私はいつもお母さんの側についてきた。そしてお母さんもいつも私の味方をしてくれた。それなのにお母さんは、ほとんど何の説明もなしに、私をお父さんと一緒に、まるで生ゴミか何かみたいにあっさり捨ててしまった。私はそれですごく参ってしまって、それからずいぶん長いあいだ母親のことが許せなかったの。私はお母さんにずいぶん何度も手紙を書いて、何があったのか事情を説明してほしいと頼んだ。でも彼女は私のそんな訴えかけに、一度も答えてくれなかった。私に会いたいとすら書いてこなかった」

彼女が母親に再会したのは、三年後のことである。親戚の葬儀の席だった。その頃には娘は自立して一人で暮らしていた。両親が離婚したとき、大学二年生だった彼女はそのまま家を出た。それから大学を卒業し、エレクトーンの教師の職に就いた。一方母親は、受験予備校で英語を教えていた。

Her mother confessed that she hadn't been able to talk to her own daughter because she hadn't known what to say. "I myself couldn't tell ❶where things were going," the mother said, "but the whole thing started over that pair of shorts."

"Shorts?" She'd been as startled as I was. She'd never wanted to speak to her mother ever again, but ❷curiosity got the better of her. In their mourning dress, mother and daughter went into a nearby coffee shop and ordered iced tea. She had to hear this—❸pardon the expression—this short story.

*

The shop that sold the lederhosen was in a small town an hour away by train from Hamburg. Her mother's sister ❹looked it up for her.

"All the Germans I know say if you're going to buy lederhosen, this is the place. The craftsmanship is good, and the prices aren't so expensive," said her sister.

So the mother boarded a train to buy her husband his souvenir lederhosen. In her train ❺compartment sat a middle-aged German couple, who ❻conversed with her in halting English. "I go now to buy lederhosen for souvenir," the mother said. "❼Vat shop you go to?" the couple asked. The mother named the name of the shop, and the middle-aged German couple ❽chimed in together, "❾Zat is ze place, *jah*. It is ze best." Hearing this, the mother felt very confi-

---

❶where things were going: 物事がどこに進んでいるのか   ❷curiosity got the better of her: 好奇心が彼女に勝った   ❸pardon the expression: そう呼ばしてもらえるなら   ❹looked it up: それを調べてくれた   ❺compartment: 向かい合せで座席のある車室❻conversed with her in halting English: たどたどしい英語で彼女と会話を交わした   ❼Vat: =What。いかにもドイツなまりに見える。   ❽chimed in together: 揃って口を挟んだ   ❾Zat is ze place, jah.: ★視覚方言が用いられた文。ZatはThat。zeはthe。jahはyes。全文で、「その店こそ、あなたの探している店だ」

私が、あなたに何も説明することができなかったのは、いったい何を
どのように説明すればいいのか、さっぱり見当がつかなかったからな
の、と母親は打ち明けた。「いったい何が持ち上がっているのか、それ
すら私にはよくわからなかったの」と母親は言った。「でもそもそもの
きっかけは、あの半ズボンだったと思う」

　「半ズボン？」と彼女は —— 僕がそうしたのと同じように —— びっ
くりして聞き返した。もう母親とは一生口をきかない、と彼女は心を決
めていた。しかし好奇心が彼女を捉えることになった。喪服を着た母と
娘は近所の喫茶店に入って、アイスティーを注文した。彼女は何はとも
あれ、この短い物語（というべきか）をひととおり聞かないわけにはいか
なかったのだ。

＊

　レーダーホーゼンを売る店は、ハンブルクから一時間ばかり行った、
小さな町にあった。母親の妹がその店を調べてくれた。

　「ドイツ人の知り合いにいろいろと尋ねてみたんだけど、このあたり
でレーダーホーゼンを買うのなら、そこがいちばん良いということだっ
たわ。縫製技術は確かだし、値段も妥当だって」と妹は言った。

　そこで母親は列車に乗って、夫のお土産のレーダーホーゼンを買うべ
くその町まで行った。列車のコンパートメントで、中年のドイツ人夫婦
と同席した。彼らはつたない英語を使って、母親に話しかけてきた。
「私は今から、お土産用のレーダーホーゼンを買いにいくんです」と母親
は彼らに説明した。「どこの店に行くつもりですかね？」と二人は尋ね
た。彼女はその店の名前を教えた。ドイツ人夫婦は声を揃えて言った。
「それはよろしい。ヤー、その店なら大丈夫です」。それを聞いて母親は

の意。

dent.

It was a delightful early-summer afternoon and a **❶**quaint old-fashioned town. Through the middle of the town flowed a babbling brook, its banks **❷**lush and green. Cobblestone streets led in all directions, and cats were everywhere. The mother stepped into a café for a bite of **❸***Käsekuchen* and coffee.

She was on her last sip of coffee and playing with the shop cat when the owner came over to ask what brought her to their little town. She said lederhosen, **❹**whereupon the owner pulled out a pad of paper and drew a map to the shop.

"Thank you very much," the mother said.

How wonderful it was to travel by oneself, she thought as she walked along the cobblestones. In fact, this was the first time in her fifty-five years that she had traveled alone. During the whole trip, she had not once been lonely or afraid or bored. Every scene that met her eyes was fresh and new; everyone she met was friendly. Each experience **❺**called forth emotions that had been slumbering in her, untouched and unused. What she had held **❻**near and dear until then—husband and home and daughter—was on the other side of the earth. She felt no need to **❼**trouble herself over them.

She found the lederhosen shop without problem. It was a tiny

---

❶ quaint: 古風で趣のある、美しく優雅な　❷ lush: 青々と茂った、みずみずしい　❸ *Käsekuchen*: ★ドイツでポピュラーなチーズケーキ。　❹ whereupon: そこで、ただちに　❺ called forth emotions that had been slumbering in her: 彼女の中で眠っていた（slumbering）感情を呼び起こした　❻ near and dear: 近しい、大切な　★決まり文句。　❼ trouble herself over . . .: 〜のことを気に病む［思い煩う］

満足した。

　心地よい初夏の午後だった。町はこぢんまりとした、昔風のたたずまいを保っていた。町の中央を流れの速い川が横切っており、その堤は瑞々しい緑に彩られていた。丸石敷きの街路があちこちに延び、いたるところに猫の姿が見えた。母親はカフェで休んで、コーヒーを飲み、チーズ菓子を食べた。

　コーヒーの最後の一口をすすりながら、店の猫と遊んでいると、カフェの主人がやってきて、どのようなご用向きでこの町に見えたのでしょうと尋ねた。レーダーホーゼンを買いにきたのだと彼女が答えると、主人は紙を一枚とって、その店までの地図を描いてくれた。

　「どうもご親切に」と母親は言った。

　一人で旅行するというのはなんて楽しいのだろう、彼女は丸石敷きの小道を歩きながらそう思った。考えてみれば、五十五歳の今に至るまで、一人旅をしたことなんて一度もなかったのだ。ドイツを旅行している間、彼女はただの一度も寂しいとも怖いとも思わなかったし、退屈もしなかった。目を捉えるすべての光景が新鮮であり、新奇なものだった。旅先で出会った人々はみんな親切だった。ひとつひとつの体験が、彼女の中にそれまで手つかずで埋もれていた生き生きとした感情を呼び起こした。それまで彼女がいちばん近しく、大事に感じていたものは —— 夫と家庭と娘は —— 地球の反対側にあった。それらはもう頭にも浮かばない。

　レーダーホーゼンを売る店はすぐに見つかった。古くて小さな、いか

old guild shop. It didn't have a big sign for tourists, but inside she could see scores of lederhosen. She opened the door and walked in.

Two old men worked in the shop. They spoke in a whisper as they took down measurements and scribbled them into a notebook. Behind a curtain divider was a larger work space; **❶**the monotone of sewing machines could be heard.

🎧**B87**

"**❷***Darf ich Ihnen helfen, Madame?*" the larger of the two old men **❸**addressed the mother.

"I want to buy lederhosen," she responded in English.

"Ziss make problem." The old man chose his words with care. "Ve do not make **❹**article for customer who not exist."

"My husband exist," the mother said with confidence.

"*Jah, jah*, your husband exist, of course, of course," the old man responded hastily. "Excuse my not good English. Vat I **❺**vant say, if your husband not exist here, ve cannot sell ze lederhosen."

🎧**B88**

"Why?" the mother asked, perplexed.

"Is store policy. **❻***Ist unser Prinzip*. Ve must see ze lederhosen how it fit customer, ve **❼**alter very nice, only zen ve sell. Over one hundred years ve are in business, ve build reputation on ziss policy."

"But I spend half day to come from Hamburg to buy your lederhosen."

---

❶the monotone of sewing machines could be heard: ミシンの単調な音が聞こえていた **❷**Darf ich Ihnen helfen, Madame?: ★May I help you, Madame?（いらっしゃいませ）を意味するドイツ語。 **❸**address: ～に向かって言う **❹**article: 品物 **❺**Vant: =want to **❻**Ist unser Prinzip.: ★ドイツ語で、"（It）is our Principle."（それが我々の方針です）の意。 **❼**alter: 寸法を直す

にも職人風の店だった。ツーリスト向けの派手な看板は出ていないが、店の中にレーダーホーゼンがずらりと並んでいるのが見えた。彼女はドアを開けて、中に入った。

　店の中では二人の老人が仕事をしていた。彼らはひそひそと囁くように話しながら、寸法を測り、ノートブックにそれを書き留めていた。カーテンの仕切りの向こうは、広い作業場になっている。

　「Darf ich Ihnen helfen, Madame?（何かをお求めでしょうか、マダム）」、二人の老人のうちの大柄な方が母親に尋ねた。

　「私はレーダーホーゼンを買いにきました」と母親は英語で言った。

　「それはちっと問題を作ります」と老人は苦労して言葉を選びながら言った。「私たちは実在しないお客様のために品物は作らんのです」

　「私の夫は実在しています」と母親はきっぱりと言った。

　「ヤー、ヤー、あなたの夫は実在する。もちろん、もちろん」、老人はあわてて言った。「私の英語が悪くて失礼だった。しかし私どもが言いたいのは、ここに存在しない人のためにレーダーホーゼンをお売りはできんということです」

　「どうしてですか？」と母親は面食らって質問した。

　「それが私どもの店の方針なのです。Ist unser Prinzip.お客様が私どものレーダーホーゼンをおはきになり、それをこの目で見ます。どんな具合か見ます。それから私どもはとてもじょうずに寸法を直します。そこで初めてお売りできます。私どもは当地で百年以上にわたって商売をしております。この方針で、私どもは店の評判を築いてきたのです」

　「でも私は半日かけて、わざわざハンブルクからここまでやってきたんですよ。あなたのお店でレーダーホーゼンを買うために」

"Very sorry, madame," said the old man, looking very sorry indeed. "Ve make no exception. Ziss vorld is very uncertain vorld. Trust is difficult ❶sink to earn but easy sink to lose."

🎧 **B89**

The mother sighed and stood in the doorway. She ❷racked her brain for some way to break the ❸impasse. The larger old man explained the situation to the smaller old man, who nodded sadly, *jah, jah*. Despite their great difference in size, the two old men ❹wore identical expressions.

"Well, perhaps, can we do this?" the mother proposed. "I find man just like my husband and bring him here. That man puts on lederhosen, you alter very nice, you sell lederhosen to me."

🎧 **B90**

The first old man looked her in the face, ❺aghast.

"But, madame, zat is against rule. Is not same man who tries ze lederhosen on, your husband. And ve know ziss. Ve cannot do ziss."

"Pretend you do not know. You sell lederhosen to that man and that man sell lederhosen to me. That way, ❻there is no shame to your policy. Please, I beg you. I may never come back to Germany. If I do not buy lederhosen now, I will never buy lederhosen."

🎧 **B91**

"Hmph," the old man ❼pouted. He thought for a few seconds, then turned to the other old man and spoke a stream of German.

---

❶sink: =thing　❷racked her brain: 知恵を絞った　❸impasse: 袋小路、行き詰まり　❹wore identical expressions: 同じ表情を浮かべていた　❺aghast: ぎょっとして　❻there is no shame to . . .: 〜に傷がつくことはない　❼pouted: 唇をとがらせた

「申し訳なく思います」と老人は本当に申し訳なさそうに言った。「しかし例外は作れません。この世界はとびっきり不確かな場所でありまして、信用を築き上げるのには時間がかかりますが、それを壊すのはわずかな間です」

　母親は戸口に立ったままため息をついた。そしてどうすればこの窮状を打開できるものか、懸命に頭を働かせた。大柄な老人は、小柄な老人に向かってドイツ語で事情を説明した。小柄な老人は悲しい顔をして「ヤー、ヤー」と頷いていた。体格にはずいぶん差があったが、二人の顔立ちはまるで双子のようによく似ていた。

　「それでは、こういうのはどうでしょう？」と母親は提案した。「私の夫と同じくらいの体型の人を見つけて、ここに連れてきます。その人に実際にレーダーホーゼンをはいてもらって、あなたがたがその寸法を直します。そして私にそのレーダーホーゼンを売る」

　「しかしマダム、それは方針に背きます。レーダーホーゼンをはく人は、あなたの夫ではない。その事実を私どもは知っております。それは無理な相談です」

　「事情を知らないふりをしてればいいんです。あなたはただレーダーホーゼンをその人に売ります。その人は私にレーダーホーゼンを売ります。そうすれば、おたくの信用に傷はつきません。そうでしょう？　お願い。ほんの少しだけ目をつぶってください。私はもう二度とドイツには来られないかもしれません。そうしたら、一生レーダーホーゼンを買うこともできなくなってしまいます」

　「ふうん」、老人はむずかしい顔をした。そしてしばらく頭をひねっていたが、もう一人の老人の方を向いて、早口のドイツ語でなにやらまく

They spoke back and forth several times. Then, finally, the large man turned back to the mother and said, "Very well, madame. As exception—very exception, you please understand—ve vill know nossink of ziss matter. Not so many come from Yapan to buy leder-hosen, and ve Germans not so **❶**slow in ze head. Please find man very like your husband. My brother he says ziss."

"Thank you," she said. Then she managed to thank the other brother in German: "**❷***Das ist so nett von Ihnen.*"

🎧 B92

She—the daughter who's telling me this story—folds her hands on the table and sighs. I drink the last of my coffee, **❸**long since cold. The rain keeps coming down. Still no sign of my wife. Who'd have ever thought the conversation would **❹**take this turn?

"So then?" I **❺**interject, eager to hear the conclusion. "Did your mother end up finding someone with the same build as your fa-ther?"

"Yes," she says, utterly without expression. "Mother sat on a bench looking for someone who matched Father's size. **❻**And along came a man who fit the part. Without asking his permission—it seems the man couldn't speak a word of English—she dragged him

---

❶slow in ze head: 機転がきかない　❷*Das ist so nett von Ihnen.*: ★ドイツ語で、That's very kind of you. (ご親切にありがとう)。フォーマルなお礼の言葉。soは、英語のsoと同じく強調の副詞。
❸long since cold: とっくに冷めてしまった　❹take this turn: (会話が) このような方向に展開する　❺interject: 口を挟む　❻And along came a man who fit the part:「そして、その役割にぴったりの男性がやってきた」。ここでは倒置表現が使われている。

したてた。二人はひとしきりあれこれ言い合っていた。それからやっと大柄な老人が母親の方に向き直った。そして言った、「わかりました、マダム。これは今度だけの例外です —— 例外中の例外ですぞ。そのことはご理解くださいませ。私どもは何ひとつ知らんということにします。日本からわざわざレーダーホーゼンを買いにみえる方が、数多くいらっしゃるわけではありません。そして私どもドイツ人も、救いなく頭が固いわけではありません。あなたのご主人になるべくそっくりの背格好の人を捜してきてください。兄も、それでかまわないと申しております」

「ありがとう」と彼女は言った。それからお兄さんに向かってドイツ語で言った。「Das ist so nett von Ihnen.（ご親切を感謝します）」

彼女は —— つまりこの話を僕に語っている娘は —— テーブルの上で両手を重ねてため息をつく。僕はすっかり冷たくなってしまったコーヒーの残りを飲む。雨は降りやまない。妻はまだ買い物から戻ってこない。どこからどうして、こんな話になってしまったのだろう？

「それから、どうなったの？」、僕は結末を知りたくて、先を促す。「君のお母さんは、お父さんと同じくらいの背格好の人をうまく見つけることができたの？」

「うん」と彼女は表情のない顔で答える。「お母さんは外のベンチに座って、お父さんと同じような体型をした男の人を探したわけ。そこにまさにぴったりの人が通りかかった。お母さんは説明もなしに、ほとんど無理矢理に —— というのは相手は英語がぜんぜんしゃべれなかったからなんだけど —— その人をレーダーホーゼンの店までひっぱって

to the lederhosen shop."

🎧B93

"**❶**The hands-on approach," I joke.

"I don't know. At home, Mother was always **❷**a normal sensible-shoes woman," she said with another sigh. "The shopkeepers explained the situation to the man, and the man gladly consented to **❸**stand in for Father. He puts the lederhosen on, and they're pulling here and tucking there, the three of them **❹**chortling away in German. In thirty minutes the job was done, during which time Mother made up her mind to divorce Father."

🎧B94

"Wait," I say, "I don't get it! Did something happen during those thirty minutes?"

"Nothing at all. Only those three German men **❺***ha-ha-ha*-ing like bellows."

"But what made your mother do it?"

"That's something even Mother herself didn't understand at the time. It made her **❻**defensive and confused. All she knew was, looking at that man in the lederhosen, she felt an unbearable disgust rising in her. Directed toward Father. And she could not hold it back. Mother's lederhosen man, **❼**apart from the color of his skin, was exactly like Father, the shape of the legs, the belly, the thinning hair. The way he was so happy trying on those new lederhosen, all

---

❶The hands-on approach: 実践的なやり方　❷a normal sensible-shoes woman:★直訳すると「実用的な靴をはくタイプのふつうの女性」。　❸stand in for . . .: ～の代理を務める❹chortling away: 愉しげに笑って　❺*ha-ha-ha*-ing like bellows: ふいご (bellows) のように高らかに笑って　❻defensive: 神経過敏な、ぴりぴりした　❼apart from . . .: ～は別にして

いった」

「ずいぶん大胆な人みたいだ」と僕は感心して言った。

「よくわからないのよ。家にいたときには、すごくおっとりしていて、引っ込み思案な人みたいに見えたんだけど」と彼女はまたため息をつく。「店の人に前後の事情を説明され、その男の人は、わかりました、そういうことならと言って、快くお父さんのかわりをつとめてくれた。彼はレーダーホーゼンをはいて、老人たちはそのあちこちを短くしたり、詰めたりした。そしてそのあいだ三人は和気あいあいとドイツ語で冗談を言い合っていた。作業は30分ほどで終わった。そしてその作業が終わるころには、お母さんはもう離婚しようと心を決めていたの」

「ちょっと待って」と僕は言う。「もうひとつよくわからないんだけど、その30分のあいだに何か特別なことが起こったわけ？」

「いいえ、べつに何も起こらなかった。三人のドイツ人がただにこやかにおしゃべりをしていただけ」

「じゃあいったい、何がお母さんに離婚の決心をさせたんだろう？」

「お母さんにもそれはわからなかった。そのときにはね。いったい何がどうなっているのか自分でもつかめなくて、すっかり頭が混乱してしまった。彼女にわかるのは、そのレーダーホーゼンをはいた男の姿を眺めているうちに、耐えがたいほどの嫌悪感が自分の中にわき起こってきた、ということだけだった。父親に対する嫌悪感がね。そしてそれをどこかに押しやることは、彼女にはできなかった。そのレーダーホーゼンをはいた男は、肌の色を除けば、父親にほとんどそっくりだったの。脚のかたちから、お腹の出具合から、髪の薄くなり方まで。彼は新しい

❶prancy and cocky like a little boy. As Mother stood there looking at this man, so many things she'd been uncertain of about herself slowly shifted together into something very clear. That's when she realized she hated Father."

🎧B95

My wife gets home from shopping, and the two of them commence their woman talk, but I'm still thinking about the lederhosen. The three of us eat an early dinner and have a few drinks; I keep turning the story over in my mind.

🎧B96

"So, you don't hate your mother anymore?" I ask when my wife leaves the room.

"No, not really. We're not close at all, but I ❷don't hold anything against her."

"Because she told you about the lederhosen?"

"I think so. After she explained things to me, I couldn't go on hating her. I can't say why it makes any difference, I certainly don't know how to explain it, but it may have something to do with us being women."

"Still, ❸if you leave the lederhosen out of it, ❹supposing it was just the story of a woman taking a trip and finding herself, would you have been able to forgive her?"

"Of course not," she says without hesitation. "❺The whole point

---

❶prancy and cocky: ★prancyもcockyも上機嫌にはしゃいでいる感じ。　❷don't hold anything against her: 彼女には何の恨みもない　❸if you leave the lederhosen out of it: ★直訳は「そこからレーダーホーゼンの要素を外すと」。leave A out of Bで、「AをBから除外する」。　❹supposing . . .: もし〜としたら　❺The whole point: 核心、肝心なこと

レーダーホーゼンを試着しながら、とても楽しそうだった。意気揚々と
して、得意げだった。まるで小さな子供みたいに。そこに立って、その
男の様子を見ているうちに、これまで彼女の中でぼんやりとしていたい
くつかのものごとが、すごくありありとかたちをとり始めた。そこで彼女
にはやっとわかったの。自分が今では夫を憎んでいるんだってことが」

　妻が買い物からやっと戻ってきて、二人は女同士のおしゃべりを始め
る。でも僕はまだそのレーダーホーゼンの話のことを考えている。三人
で早い目の夕食を食べ、お酒を少し呑む。それでもその話は僕の頭を離
れない。
　「それで、君はもうお母さんに腹は立てていないの？」、妻が席を外し
たときに、彼女にそう尋ねてみる。
　「そうね。元通り仲良くなれたっていうわけじゃないのよ。でも少な
くとも腹は立てていないと思う」
　「それはレーダーホーゼンの話を聞かされたから？」
　「たぶん。その話を聞いたあとでは、私の中にあった母親に対する激
しい怒りみたいなものは、消えてしまっていた。どうしてそうなってし
まったのか、一口では言えない。でもそれは、私たちが女どうしだって
ことと関係しているのかもしれないわね」
　「でもさ、もしそこにレーダーホーゼンが出てこなかったら ── つま
り女の人が一人旅をして、そこでこれまでになかった自分を発見して
── というような話だけだったとしたら、君はお母さんのことを許せ
たと思う？」
　「もちろん許せなかったでしょうね」と彼女は躊躇なく答える。「重要

is the lederhosen, right?"

❶A proxy pair of lederhosen, I'm thinking, that her father never even received.

—translated by Alfred Birnbaum

❶A proxy pair of lederhosen: 身代わりのレーダーホーゼン

なのはレーダーホーゼンなのよ。わかる？」

　その身代わりのレーダーホーゼンを、お父さんは受け取りさえしな
かったのだ、と僕は思う。

Authors & Translator

ティム・オブライエン
1946年ミネソタ州生まれ。大学卒業後に従軍したベトナム戦争をテーマに、作品を発表し続けている。戦場風景をリアルに描いた初期作品から、マジックリアリズム的な『カチアートを追跡して』(*Going After Cacciato*, 1978)、ベトナム戦争とは一見無関係な *Tomcat in Love* (1998)、『世界のすべての七月』(*July, July*, 2002) まで、作風は多岐にわたる。

———

レイモンド・カーヴァー
1938年オレゴン州生まれ。短篇小説の名手であり詩人。「ミニマリスト」と呼ばれるもととなった、描写をぎりぎりまで削ぎ落とした文体を特徴とする。日常生活の中に潜む悲哀、絶望、希望を描く『頼むから静かにしてくれ』(*Will You Please Be Quiet, Please?*, 1976) といった短篇集を残す。村上春樹訳で全集が刊行されている。1988年没。

———

村上春樹
1949年京都生まれ。『羊をめぐる冒険』(1982)、『ノルウェイの森』(1987)、『ねじまき鳥クロニクル』(1994-1995)、『海辺のカフカ』(2002)、『1Q84』(2009-2010) を代表作にもつ小説家。その一方で、オブライエン、カーヴァーのほか、J・D・サリンジャーやスコット・フィッツジェラルド、レイモンド・チャンドラーなど、多くのアメリカ作家作品の翻訳も精力的に手がけている。

Acknowledgements

ON THE RAINY RIVER／レイニー河で
From the work THE THINGS THEY CARRIED by Tim O'Brien
Copyright © 1990 by Tim O'Brien
Permission for this edition was arranged through The English Agency (Japan) Ltd.
Reprinted by permission of Houghton Mifflin Harcourt Publishing Company
『本当の戦争の話をしよう』（文藝春秋、1990）にて村上訳初出／文春文庫所収

A SMALL, GOOD THING／ささやかだけれど、役に立つこと
from CATHEDRAL
Copyright © 1983, Raymond Carver
Copyright renewed © 1989, Tess Gallagher
All rights reserved
Japanese translation © Haruki Murakami
English reprint and Japanese translation rights arranged with Tess Gallagher c/o The Wylie
Agency(UK) LTD, London through Tuttle-Mori Agency, Inc., Tokyo
『ささやかだけれど、役に立つこと』（中央公論社、1989）にて村上訳初出／『Carver's Dozen—レ
イモンド・カーヴァー傑作選』（中公文庫）所収

LEDERHOSEN／レーダーホーゼン
Copyright © Haruki Murakami, 1985, 2005
English copyright © Haruki Murakami, 1992
Translated from Japanese into English by Alfred Birnbaum
英訳は「グランタ」1992年冬号にて初出／『象の消滅—短篇選集1980-1991—』（新潮社）所収

新装版

村上春樹ハイブ・リット

発行日：2008 年 11 月 30 日（初版）

　　　　2020 年 2 月 14 日（新装版）

著者：ティム・オブライエン／レイモンド・カーヴァー／村上春樹
編訳者：村上春樹
総合監修：柴田元幸
朗読者：ティム・オブライエン／グレッグ・デール（Story 2）／ジャック・マルジ（Story 3）
編集：株式会社アルク 出版編集部
AD：松田行正＋杉本聖士
発行人：田中伸明
英文校正：Peter Branscombe ／ Owen Schaefer ／ Joel Weinberg
DTP：株式会社秀文社
印刷所：シナノ印刷株式会社
CD 制作：株式会社ソニー・ミュージックソリューションズ

発行所：株式会社アルク
〒 102-0073　東京都千代田区九段北 4-2-6　市ヶ谷ビル
Website：https://www.alc.co.jp/

Printed in Japan © Tim O'Brien, Raymond Carver, and Haruki Murakami

PC：7019060　ISBN：978-4-7574-3387-8　C0098

地球人ネットワークを創る

アルクのシンボル
「地球人マーク」です。